GRACE
GIVERS

Grace Givers

Unless otherwise indicated, Scripture quotations used in this book are from
The New King James Version. Copyright © 1979, 1980, 1982. Thomas Nelson, Inc.

Scripture quotations marked NIV from the *Holy Bible, New International Version*®.
Copyright © 1973, 1978, 1984 by International Bible Society. Used by permission
of Zondervan Publishing House. All rights reserved.

Scripture quotations marked NLT are taken from the *Holy Bible, New Living Translation*,
copyright © 1996. Used by permission of Tyndale House Publishers, Inc.,
Wheaton, Illinois 60189. All rights reserved.

Cover and Interior Design: Greg Jackson, Thinkpen Design, LLC

ISBN 1-59145-483-2

Printed in the United States of America

06 07 08 09 QWB 6 5 4 3 2 1

*Stories of People Who
Have Been Captured by Grace–and
Are Sharing It with the World*

GRACE
GIVERS

INTEGRITY
HOUSE™

DR. DAVID JEREMIAH

Table of Contents

Introduction

WHAT HAPPENS WHEN SOMEONE IS CAPTURED BY GRACE?

Someone has written that grace is a five-letter word that is often spelled J-E-S-U-S.... He was the once-and-for-all perfect human image of grace, of love, of truth. "In the beginning was the Word, and the Word was with God, and the Word was God.... And the Word became flesh and dwelt among us, and we beheld His glory, the glory as of the only begotten of the Father, full of grace and truth.... For the law was given through Moses, but grace and truth came through Jesus Christ" (John 1:1, 14, 17).

In the Greek tongue of Paul's day, the word for "grace" was *charis*. It carried the connotation of graciousness or favor. But the term evolved in the Greek world until it meant the actual gift, the concrete expression of kindness. Grace happens. As Paul explained it, "The free gift is not like the offense. For if by the one man's offense many died, much more the grace of God and the gift by the grace of the one Man, Jesus Christ, abounded to many" (Romans 5:15).

Grace happens, and it acts. "For by grace you have been saved through faith, and that not of yourselves, it is the gift of God" (Ephesians 2:8).

Such grace can come only from God. It is the gift unsought, unmerited, unlimited. For no matter what we have done, no matter the depth of our transgression, the darkness of our hearts—grace overrules them all. God pursues us relentlessly, He will not give us up, and once He has captured us, He won't let us go.

In the following pages, you'll find stories of people who have been pursued by God, captured by His grace—and are now sharing that grace with the world. When grace happens in our lives, it cannot be contained. It must spill into the lives of those around us. As you read, may you find yourself captured by grace and transformed into a grace giver.

*approaches him just as he is.
Grace does not wait till there is
something to attract it nor till
a good·reason is found in the
sinner for its flowing to him.*

HORATIUS BONAR

Grace Givers Know How Much They've Been Forgiven

But God, who is rich in mercy, because of His great love with which He loved us, even when we were dead in trespasses, made us alive together with Christ (by grace you have been saved).

EPHESIANS 2:4-5

Even the selfish, calculating Prodigal cannot withstand the sight of his running, weeping father surrendering his high position to meet him at the edge of disgrace. In that moment grace takes him captive, and he sees what his rebellious soul has not until now allowed him to see: the beauty of his father's love, the absolute value of his acceptance, the sweet joys of loyalty and obedience. As far as his conscience goes, no one need tell him the depth of the pain he has brought to his home. He knows it now not simply with his mind but in the furthest depths of his heart. The heart is broken, yet his soul is mended. Such is the supernatural event of grace.

*Humanity is never so beautiful
as when praying for forgiveness,
or else forgiving one another.*

JEAN PAUL RICHTER

His Grace Is Sufficient

DAVID JEREMIAH

On the morning of Sunday, November 8, 1987, Irishman Gordon Wilson and his twenty-eight-year-old daughter, Marie, went to watch a parade in the town of Enniskillen in Northern Ireland. As they stood beside a brick wall waiting for units of British soldiers and police to come marching by, an IRA terrorist bomb exploded behind them.

A half-dozen people were killed instantly by the blast, and Gordon and his daughter were buried several feet deep beneath a pile of bricks. Gordon could feel injuries to his shoulder and arm, but was unable to move. Then he felt someone touch his fingers.

"Is that you, Dad?" Marie whispered. "Yes, Marie," her father answered. He heard the muffled sounds of people screaming from pain, and then the much clearer sound of Marie's screams. He squeezed her hand tightly, repeatedly asking her if she was all right. Between her screams of pain, she repeatedly assured her father that she was okay.

"Daddy, I love you very much," were the last words Gordon Wilson heard his daughter say. Four hours later, after they were finally rescued, she died in a hospital from massive brain and spinal injuries.

Later that evening, a BBC reporter asked to speak with Gordon. After he described what had happened, the reporter asked him, "How do you feel about the guys who planted the bomb?"

His words were stunning. "I bear them no ill will," Gordon replied. "I bear them no grudge. Bitter talk is not going to bring Marie Wilson back to life. I shall pray tonight and every night that God will forgive them." Some speculate that it was that statement that soothed paramilitary groups incensed by the bombing, thereby preventing a bloody retaliatory attack.

In the ensuing months, many people asked Gordon, who eventually became a senator in the Republic of Ireland, how he could forgive such a murderous act of hatred.

"I was hurt," Gordon said. "I had just lost my daughter. but I wasn't angry. Marie's last words to me—words of love—had put me on a plane of love. *I received God's grace, through the strength of His love for me, to forgive"* (italics added). For years after the tragedy that took his daughter's life and almost his own, Gordon Wilson worked tirelessly for peace and reconciliation in Northern Ireland until his own death.

Gordon Wilson had experienced God's grace, His all-pervading love and forgiveness. When that grace touches our lives, we feel forgiven and free at the core of our being, and we find the grace to forgive others. And that kind of grace and forgiveness can bring peace where there is strife, healing where there is despair. That kind of grace can change our lives and the lives of those around us—even those who hurt us—forever. ✺

Therefore be imitators of God as dear children. And walk in love, as Christ also has loved us and given Himself for us, an offering and a sacrifice to God for a sweet-smelling aroma.

EPHESIANS 5:1-2

> *To excuse what can really produce*
> *good excuses is not Christian charity;*
> *it is only fairness. To be a Christian*
> *means to forgive the inexcusable,*
> *because God has forgiven*
> *the inexcusable in you.*
>
> C. S. LEWIS

I Simply Let Go

KAREN O'CONNOR

It is better to forgive too much than to condemn too much.

ANONYMOUS

I thought about her. I dreamed about her. I saw her in every woman I met. Some even had her name, *Cathy*. Others had her deep-set blue eyes or curly dark hair. Even the slightest resemblance turned my stomach into a knot.

Weeks, months, years passed. Was I never to be free of this woman who had pursued my husband, Jack, then married him following our divorce? My resentment, guilt, and anger were draining me, and I went about my days without a spark of life. I tried everything to get free. I went into counseling. I attended self-help classes and enrolled in seminars and workshops. I read books. I talked to anyone who would listen.

I ran. I walked the beach. I drove for miles to nowhere. I screamed into my pillow at night. I prayed. I blamed myself. I did everything I knew how to do—except surrender.

Before she came into my life, my days were simple, predictable, and filled with good things, the stuff most women long for: a successful husband, children I loved, tennis with my friends three mornings a week, church on Sundays, summer vacations, a lovely home, and a beautiful car. What more could I have wanted?

Now suddenly everything was different. My life would never be the same again. I hated the man I had loved for over twenty years—my husband, the father of my children. I hated the other woman. And I was beginning to hate myself. *How can any good come from such pain and grief?* I asked over and over. How would we carry on?

I did not receive an answer right away. But one Saturday, a church in my neighborhood held a day-long seminar on the healing power of forgiveness, and I felt somehow drawn to the event. After the introduction and some discussion and sharing, the leader invited participants to close their eyes and picture someone in their lives they had not forgiven, for whatever reason. Cathy's name loomed large in my mind.

Next, he asked whether or not we'd be willing to forgive that person, and I went cold. How could I forgive a person like Cathy? She not only had hurt me—she'd hurt my children as well. Unforgivable.

Then I sensed God's gentle voice within: *Are you ready to let go of this? To release her?*

I was certain everyone around me could hear my heart beating. Yes, I was willing. I couldn't hold on to my anger any longer. It was killing me. And in that moment, without doing anything else, an incredible shift occurred within me—I simply let go.

For the first time since my husband had left, I gave control of my life over to the Lord. I released my grip on Cathy, on Jack, and on myself. I let go of my rage and resentment.

How self-righteous I had been. How judgmental. How important it had been for me to be right, no matter what the cost. And it had cost me plenty—my health, my spontaneity, my vitality, my sense of closeness with God.

That night I slept straight through until morning. No dreams. No haunting face. No reminders.

If it had been up to me alone, I don't know if I would have had the courage or the generosity to make the first move. But it was not up to me. There was no mistaking the power of the Holy Spirit within me.

The following Monday, I walked into my office and wrote Cathy a letter. The words spilled onto the page without effort.

"Dear Cathy," I began. I proceeded to tell her what had occurred during the seminar. I also told her how I had hated her for what she had done to my marriage and to my family, and, as a result, how I had denied both of us the healing power of forgiveness. I apologized for my hateful thoughts and offered her forgiveness. I signed my name, slipped the letter into an envelope, and popped it in the mailbox—without looking back.

On Wednesday afternoon, the phone rang.

"Karen?"

There was no mistaking the voice.

"It's Cathy," she said softly.

I was surprised that my stomach remained calm. My hands were dry. My voice was steady and sure. I listened more than I talked—which was unusual for me. I found myself actually interested in what Cathy had to say.

She thanked me for the letter, and she acknowledged my courage in writing it. Then she told me how sorry she was—for everything. She talked briefly about her regret, her sadness for me, for my children, and more. All I had ever wanted to hear from her, she said that day.

As I replaced the receiver, however, another insight came to me. I realized that as nice as it was to hear her words of apology, they paled in comparison to what God was teaching me. Buried deep in the trauma of my divorce was the truth I had been looking for all my life without even knowing it: God is my source, my strength, my very supply. He alone can bring about lasting healing. He alone can bring peace to my soul and peace to my world. ✿

Do not repay evil with evil
or insult with insult,
but with blessing, because
to this you were called
so that you may
inherit a blessing.

1 PETER 3:9

The law breaks the hard heart,
but the gospel melts it.
A stone duly broken, may be still
a hard stone; but the gospel melts.

RALPH ERSKINE

When I Was a Prodigal Son

DON HALL AS TOLD TO NANETTE THORSEN-SNIPES

*A*t seventeen, I found myself sitting in a jail cell, wondering how things could have gone so wrong in my life. I didn't know it then, but looking back, I felt a lot like the Prodigal Son in the Bible. How had I gotten here? Where did I begin to go wrong?

It was two days after Thanksgiving. Clouds were slung low across the sky and pregnant with rain that cold day a few years earlier. My mom, my stepdad, Jim, and my younger brother and sister had gone to the grocery store. Before they got home, the phone rang.

After asking for my mother, the person on the phone said, "Tell her that Benny hanged himself." It felt as though someone struck me in the gut. Benny was my dad.

"Is he dead?" I asked, holding my breath and hoping it wasn't true. I couldn't cry. But the pain left an empty hole in me because I didn't know him. When the answer came back "Yes," I sat down to absorb what had happened.

A flood of memories came back. It seemed like a rerun of one of those unbelievable, yet true stories on TV. My mother had faced my dad's rage one weekend—at the business end of a gun. She finally talked him into putting it down. After he went to work, she packed our bags and moved us out. My brother was seven and I was only four, but I vividly remember that motel room where we hid for a week. I had on my cowboy outfit that day, and Mom was crying.

Maybe that's one reason why I stayed angry all those years. I was angry at my father for trying to hurt Mom. And then I was angry because he died before I could get to know him.

My anger only grew as the years passed. There were days I made life miserable for Mom and Jim by drinking. But the alcohol brought on more anger, which made me lose my temper. I put my fist through the living room wall and kicked in the bathroom door. I was arrested several times for driving under the influence.

One day, I became angry because the bike I'd bought with my hard-earned money wouldn't work right. I picked up the ten-speed bicycle and began screaming obscenities. I slammed it repeatedly into the ground until it lay in a crumpled heap.

Mom and Jim became alarmed at my uncontrollable rage and took me to see a counselor. I had nothing to say to a shrink. I just sat there and waited for him to quit talking. After the third session, he gave up and told Mom he couldn't help me if I wouldn't communicate, which suited me just fine.

My drinking worsened and I had bouts with depression, staying in bed for days. I also started hanging out with bad company, and earned myself some dangerous enemies.

One day a bullet hit my car as I drove down the highway. I think it was kids from a rival school. When someone kicked down the basement door which led to my bedroom, I got scared. I guess that's why I took the gun from my parents' closet. I never kept it loaded, but its presence made me feel safe.

The next evening, I drove to the hotel where my brother worked. After parking my car, I went straight toward the bar.

Inside, a strong, burly man said, "Son, I need to see your ID." Because I didn't have one, I tried to muscle my way past the guy. He became angry and shoved me. I shoved back. The next thing I knew, he smacked me in the jaw and I hit the floor. I jumped up, waving the gun in his face.

In a split second, I heard, "Freeze!" I turned to my left where three policemen stood in a firing stance, their guns drawn and aimed directly at me. To my right, I looked down the barrel of another officer's gun. It was like I was moving in slow motion amid the chaos around me. Then an inner voice I knew was God gently prompted me to obey the officers' orders and face the wall. I did, and I was handcuffed and taken to jail.

So for the fourth or fifth time, I sat in the county jail with the stench of bodily fluids and sweaty men surrounding me. I didn't worry. Whenever I was caught driving under the influence of alcohol, my parents always posted bail for me. So I was shocked when I called for them to get me out and Mom said no.

I didn't realize at the time that they had been in prayer for me and that they'd finally let go and entrusted me to God. After a while, I knew I was in real trouble and I said a simple prayer, "God, please help me. All I want is a decent life."

A few days later, a friend and his father posted bail for me. Angrily, I went home and packed my things, never once speaking to my parents. Then I moved in with my friend.

Things turned around a few months later when I met a beautiful young woman. We later married, and now have two wonderful children. Several months after marrying, my wife and I both turned our lives over to the Lord. This prodigal son had come home.

I have a new life now, thanks to the grace of God. But sometimes I still feel regret about all the pain I caused my parents. One recent Christmas while my wife and the kids were at Mom's, Jim and I went to the grocery store. While in the cab of the truck with music softly playing in the background, I said, "Jim, can you ever forgive me for all the pain I've put you through?"

The man I knew as my dad looked at me and smiled. "I've already forgiven you, Donnie," he said. Then he put his arm around me. I couldn't help thinking of that parable once again, and how our Heavenly Father always welcomes us home. ✵

But when he was
still a great way off,
his father saw him
and had compassion,
and ran and fell on
his neck and kissed him.

LUKE 15:20

God is closest to those

with broken hearts.

JEWISH SAYING

Hospital Maneuvers

BETTY WINSLOW

When our daughter, Lisa, received an appointment to the U.S. Naval Academy, our family joined the ranks of military families throughout the ages, waiting by the phone, haunting the mailbox, living from one military leave to the next. When Lisa volunteered to be one of twenty midshipmen sent to sea during the waning days of Desert Storm, she was beside herself with excitement, but the rest of us spent the whole time praying for her safety and hoping that no uniformed stranger would knock on our door with the news no one wants to hear.

To our joy, she returned home without a scratch. We heaved a sigh of relief.

But then, on a cold December Sunday, a car pulled into the driveway, and two sober-faced naval officers got out. Lisa and three shipmates had been returning to the academy from a football game. There was a fatal car wreck; three of the shipmates had died. One of them was Lisa.

After weeks of waiting to hear the details of the accident, the news finally arrived. It had not been the driver's fault—a rotten, rain-soaked tree had fallen on or in front of the car, ripping off the roof. Our Lisa had been thrown from the car and died at the scene. The driver had been Brian, Lisa's squad leader, classmate, and good friend, and he'd been rushed to the Shock Trauma Center of the University of Maryland Medical System. He was in serious condition, and he drifted in and out of consciousness for the next few days, unable to remember anything about the accident, unaware that the girls who'd been in his care were dead.

My heart bled for the pain this young man would go through, both physical and mental, if he even survived. Three friends had died in his car. When they broke the news to him, would he be tempted to just give up and die, too, even if it wasn't his fault? Would he even be able to believe that it wasn't his fault, with no memories of it all?

I longed to go to his hospital room, hug him tightly, and tell him that he had to get better, that he had to go on living, and that, somehow, for all of us, it would be okay. I felt that this was something I needed to do, something the Lord wanted me to do—but how? Brian was in Maryland. I was in Ohio. It would cost a fortune to fly the whole family to Maryland, and there was no way I could leave my other grieving children behind. Still, I knew that if the Lord wanted me to do this, He would make it happen.

Without telling us, some of our friends had decided we needed to go to Maryland, and in no time, they had raised the money for our airplane tickets and set up transportation to and from the airport, while the Navy made housing, food, and transportation arrangements for our stay. By the time we were told about the trip, all we had to do was pack and go.

Standing outside the door to Brian's hospital room, I hesitated, suddenly unsure. Would he really want to see us? I reminded our escort, "Brian can still change his mind if he wants to."

"Yes, ma'am, he knows that. But he says he wants to see you."

When we entered his room, Brian was lying on his back, pale and still, wearing a neck brace to prevent any movement of his chipped vertebra. He was staring at the ceiling with an expression of pain and despair on his face that chilled me through and through. I silently thanked God that He had brought us here so that I could tell this young man what had been on my heart from the moment I had heard of his plight: "Live!"

Brian slowly turned his head when he realized that there were people in his room. As a well-trained future officer, he spoke first to the officers present, and they introduced him to us.

After another minute or two of conversation, my son and husband left the room and our escorting officers stepped outside to look into Brian's check-out status. Finally, Brian and I were alone.

Tears filled his eyes. Then an anguished cry broke out of him: "I'm so sorry!" I walked over to the bed and put my arms around him. As his shoulders shook with his sobs, I tried desperately not to break down myself. Brian needed me to be strong right now. I had the rest of my life to cry.

He went on and on, attacking the accident from every angle. The questions and if-only's were eating him up, magnified by his not being able to remember anything about that day.

I began to comfort him. "Even if you'd left earlier, the tree would still have fallen. It was time for Lisa to go be with Jesus. It wasn't your fault! We don't blame you, and Lisa wouldn't either."

I took his hand as we talked, and he clung tightly to it as if to a lifeline. He talked and cried for a long time as I listened and ached for him. When he finally stopped, I got up and put my arms around him again and began to pray for him. I prayed for his healing, for comfort in his grief, for his future in the Navy, and for his future relationship with God, the words pouring out of me as though God had opened a pipeline between himself and Brian, using my heart as a conduit.

After I'd prayed and we'd had a few minutes to breathe, Brian's family piled into his room to take him home. They told me how sorry they were about what happened, and I told them what I had told Brian. I knew it was important to repeat it all to them. Once Brian went home, he was going to need people around him who could remind him of what I'd said, to encourage his heart with grace.

As we left, Brian was sitting up in bed, calling for his clothes and something to eat besides hospital food. He looked like a new man—his color was better, his eyes looked less tortured, and he sounded more alert.

What was it that had turned the tide for him? The hug we'd shared? The prayer? Whatever it was, I'd done what I came to do. Brian was going to live—and live well. Now we could both start to heal. ❁

Blessed be the God and Father of our Lord Jesus Christ,
the Father of mercies and God of all comfort,
who comforts us in all our tribulation, that we may
be able to comfort those who are in any trouble.

2 CORINTHIANS 1:3-4

Don't be afraid to go out on a limb.
That's where the fruit is.

H. JACKSON BROWN

The Birthday Gift

JUDITH SCHARFENBERG

When I encountered Jesus and experienced His life-giving forgiveness, I wanted to tell the whole world that their sins could be forgiven; that they could know for sure they were going to heaven; that their lives could change and take on a new meaning and purpose. And I wanted to start with my family. Not only did I love them because they were my family, but they also needed the Lord in ways I deeply felt. My brother lived in fear and despair, and my dad was an alcoholic.

Despite my joy and my obvious love and concern for them, my attempts were pitiful, met with Mom's apathy—"That's real nice, honey"—my brother's anger, and my dad's mocking skepticism. I felt like a complete failure.

Dad was a philosopher of sorts and considered himself an authority on everything. I admired and respected him; I had always looked to him for advice. But I had found the answer to life, an answer ridiculed by the man whose opinion I'd always valued most. How would I convince him both that what I believed was true and that I still respected him?

Every time we got together, he would bring up my religious beliefs, his voice dripping with sarcasm. "So how much do you think your pastor makes? Is he like all the rest, always asking for money?" My mind would go blank. I'd tremble inside and stammer like a fool. Once, I did manage to articulate a point from the Bible, but he dismissed it with, "Judy, your stories are nice fairy tales, but there's no truth in the Bible." When I told him Jesus died and rose again, he replied, "There is no way a man can rise from the dead. It just can't be done."

After a few years, Dad became seriously ill, and I worried that time was running out. He had abused his body with tobacco and alcohol for many years, and we both knew he was not going to live to a ripe old age. He recovered, a thinner and frailer man, but just as cocky as ever.

Not long after his recovery, his birthday rolled around. As I shopped for his birthday gift, the usual shirt or tie seemed meaningless. I wanted this present to have lasting value. His hospital stay had made me aware of how uncertain the times were. What if this were his last birthday? Somewhat frantic, on an impulse I bought him a beautiful red leather Bible and had his name engraved on the cover. It was gorgeous, but as I drove home, I had second and third thoughts, wondering why I'd done such a stupid thing. He'd probably just throw it away.

I worried all the way to his party. What on earth had possessed me to buy a Bible? I knew how he'd respond—with more sarcasm. Under my breath, I prayed, "Help, Lord! Give me the courage to give this Bible to my Dad. Change his heart so he'll want to know You like I do." And with that, I knew that how my dad responded wasn't up to me.

Dinner was over and it was time for cake and presents. I said, "Daddy, now that you're retiring, what are you going to do with the rest of your life?"

His eyes lit up and he quipped, "Why, Judy, I think I'll be a preacher!"

I handed him his present and boldly said, "Well, Daddy, I know one thing. If you're going to be a preacher, you'll need a Bible!"

The grin left his face as he opened the gift. He unwrapped the box and gently took the Bible out of the tissue paper. Time seemed to stand still as he looked at his name engraved on that Bible.

My dad never teased me again. In fact, I think that Bible became very precious to him. I can't explain why, but after that, whenever I went to his house I saw the Bible next to his favorite chair. Were those cracks in the leather edges signs that it had been used?

A few months later, he left the United States. He and my stepmother planned to retire in the Philippines where her family lived. We had a big sendoff at the airport, and with a flurry of goodbyes, hugs, and kisses, they were gone. I watched my dad walk through the security gate. It was then that I recognized something in his hand—the rich burgundy of the leather Bible.

By December, he was critically ill once again. My stepmother called to tell me how sick he was. I felt helpless those thousands of miles away, but I prayed for a miracle. The second call came just four days later. Nora's faint voice said, "He's gone, Judy."

Three days later, I received a letter my father had written shortly before his death. He said that he'd never felt so weak. He wrote, "Judy, all I can do is sleep and eat and read my Bible. It's keeping me good company."

I never heard my dad pray to receive Christ. Only the Lord knows what was in his heart, what transpired those last few days, but I am comforted. My dad had been reading God's Word, and God has promised that His Word will not return void.

It was grace that forgave my sins, and grace that spurred me to share forgiveness with my family. And even though that endeavor was completely outside my capabilities, it was

God's grace that worked through me—God graciously helped a stammering, frightened new believer witness to a mocking skeptic. Because of that grace, I have hope that I will see my father in heaven. ✦

As a father pities his children,
So the LORD pities those who fear Him.
For He knows our frame;
He remembers that we are dust.

PSALM 103:13-14

Forgiveness does not change the past,
but it does enlarge the future.

PAUL BOESE

Serving Grace

DARLENE SCHACHT

O n a rainy fall day when I was a kid, my mom taught me a lesson in grace.

My dad walked through the kitchen door with the familiar yellow wallet in his hand. It was dirty, wet, and missing the twenty dollars that had been tucked inside earlier that week.

"I found it outside, right next to the trash can," he said, handing it over to my mom.

We all knew it meant two things. One, someone just wanted the money and had discarded the rest. Two, someone from our own house had taken it. The same face instantly flashed in all of our minds: that of Cindy, the girl (if you could call her that) who lived across the street. Cindy was a tomboy if ever there was one—my dad even called her Tom. She loved to help him around the yard, mending fences, cutting grass, and whacking bees' nests off the shed. I think my dad enjoyed her company, having never had a son. And I know Cindy loved being with him, having never had a father call her his own.

Her relationship with her own father was marked by the long scar that trickled sadly across her cheek, a permanent reminder of the day he threw a broken jar, hoping to erase her from his life.

Breaking the silence, my mother spoke. "My purse was behind the chair where I always keep it. Cindy is the only one who's been over this weekend," she said solemnly; and then she paused, unsure of what to do or think.

Cindy avoided our attempts at contact all day. That evening, my mom called her house, and her mother asked if there was something she could do for us. After Mom expressed her suspicion, Cindy's mom told her that Cindy had twenty dollars, but she had told her mom that it was money that was raised for the school. She also told my mom that Cindy would be over to apologize and return the money within a few minutes.

Five minutes later, Cindy was standing in our kitchen, holding twenty dollars in an open hand, avoiding eye contact with my mom.

I stared at my mom. Part of me wished we could somehow avoid the confrontation, while another part of me hoped she would give Cindy the lecture of her life. I felt a righteous anger—she had abused my friendship and robbed my family, and I knew that she needed to be punished.

Cindy was waiting to face the music. What she faced instead was grace.

Instead of a lecture, instead of harsh words, and instead of finger-pointing, my mom chose to forgive. I stood there, watching my mom wrap her arms around my friend, telling her how much she loved her and how much she meant to our family. "I forgive you," Mom said, holding her as close as her own child. Tears trickled down the scarred cheek of this young girl, and I think I caught a glimpse of her inner scars beginning to heal.

My mom had taught me about grace—about the great love and limitless forgiveness of God—all my life, and now I saw her living it. And as much as that encounter affected me, I know it affected a girl named Cindy in a much more powerful way, reaching deep into her heart with God's healing grace. ❁

Bear with each other
and forgive whatever
grievances you may have
against one another.
Forgive as the Lord
forgave you.

COLOSSIANS 3:13 NIV

*Grace binds you with far stronger cords
than the cords of duty or obligation
can bind you. Grace is free, but when
once you take it, you are bound
forever to the Giver, and bound
to catch the spirit of the Giver.
Like produces like, grace makes you
gracious, the Giver makes you give.*

E. STANLEY JONES

Graced and Gracious

DAVID JEREMIAH

Christiana Tsai, one of twenty siblings, was born to a Chinese ruling family during the Manchu dynasty. She enjoyed a good education, personal servants, and an isolated life, almost never venturing outside the walls of her family's palace. But Christiana's father, despite Buddhist convictions, wanted Christiana to attend a Christian school run by missionaries from America. "Just be sure you don't eat Christianity!" he said, meaning he didn't want his children converting to the foreign religion.

At boarding school, however, Christiana heard the Gospel and was drawn to Jesus Christ. Her conversion shocked her family. A servant was dispatched to bring her home. On the boat, he gave her a rope and a knife. "You have disgraced your family by eating the Christian religion," he told her, warning that if she did not renounce her faith, she would have "to choose between this rope to hang yourself, this knife to stab yourself, or this canal to drown yourself."

The girl, however, bore the wrath of her family, who treated her like a dog, even tearing her Bible and hymnbook to pieces.

She was threatened, punished, rejected, ridiculed, and treated with contempt by the servants. "But," Christiana later wrote, "I did not argue; I only prayed for wisdom, and God gave me grace."

One day one of her brothers said to her, "Tell me about Christianity and why you became a Christian." When Christiana told him, he replied, "That was a remarkable experience. I have noticed that in spite of the way we treat you now, you seem much happier than you used to be. I think I would like to believe, too."

In the course of time, fifty-five relatives received Jesus, including the brother who had torn up her Bible and hymnbook. Christiana Tsai found the secret of conveying to others the grace she herself had received, and it was her gracious spirit that drew her family to Christ like a magnet.

Sometimes the grace we've received doesn't flow freely into the lives of others—sometimes it becomes trapped by bitterness or distractions. But when we look to Jesus as our example, when we determine to surrender to the Lord and show grace to those who persecute us, grace doubles in our hearts and flows, unencumbered, into the hearts of those around us. ✲

*Let us therefore come boldly
to the throne of grace,
that we may obtain mercy
and find grace to help us
in our time of need.*

HEBREWS 4:16

Anger makes you smaller,
while forgiveness forces you
to grow beyond where you were.

CHERIE CARTER-SCOTT

Forgive? Who, Me?

SUZANNAH WILLINGHAM

I knew before my wedding that my relationship with my mother-in-law was going to be a tightrope walk. The first clue came when my search for a wedding dress quickly became all about what she would wear on the big day rather than what the bride would. Long after I had ruled out the few bridal gowns in a tiny boutique, she was still slowly perusing the size eight chiffons—dresses far smaller than her ample girth. It took every ounce of patience I possessed to keep from screaming, "This is about me, not you!" Little did I realize at the time that my patience was about to experience a growth spurt of necessity.

After the wedding, it didn't take long to discover my MIL, as I came to mentally call her, had all sorts of unwritten rules about just about everything. Only visits to her house counted as visits—her coming to our house did not constitute a visit and would not count the next time she wanted to complain that we hadn't visited in a while. When we had children, the definition of "visit" became even tighter: They had to visit her one at a time, and only a stay of at least three days qualified as a visit. If she gave me money to buy things for the children, I had to buy what she stipulated, not what they needed. Also, a telephone call from me was not sufficient as an invitation to our home or an event. Only a paper invitation would do. It was a high-maintenance relationship, to say the least.

At first, the relationship was merely challenging and strained. But over the years, interpreting and anticipating all these unwritten rules became extremely tedious. Sometimes they applied and sometimes not. Or occasionally there was an unexpected caveat to a rule just when I thought I had mastered it. At some point, I finally lost my cool and stopped playing the rule game. That's when the vaguely combative relationship escalated into a near war.

I always suspected I was the enemy in my MIL's eyes. After all, I'd corrupted her only son, luring him into—of all things—marriage. Now that I refused to play her games, I really became her target. Criticism was my constant companion when she was near. Nothing pleased her. Eventually, we hit an impasse that couldn't be navigated. For over a year, she refused to see us.

Finally, she wrote a letter asking for a meeting on neutral ground. If I'd known the reason for the meeting, I'd never have attended. For over an hour, she bombarded me with verbal missiles. She wounded on many levels, recalling the pain of our years of infertility and questioning if our children were really my husband's. She brought up numerous incidents where I had offended her—most of which were manufactured in her mind, or occasions where I recalled the conversation to be far different than she portrayed. The venom of her hatred and resentment of me poured forth in great torrents while my husband sat, mouth agape, across the table. But between the two of us, I was definitely the more shocked.

When her assault slowed, we made a move to leave. As we parted, she stated with quivering chin that she hoped to see us some day in a happier place. Casting a sidelong glance at me that implied her doubts as to my admission to heaven, that happier place, she benignly handed us a bag of apples, as if the visit had been cordial. My husband and I sat shell-shocked in the car for long moments. At last he whispered, "I never knew she hated you so much."

For months afterwards, I was consumed with anger. How dare she talk to me like that? She was horrible, not worthy of our love. I took long walks and cried out to God about the injustice of her words and the pain they caused me. I rehearsed awful things I wanted to say to her. I demanded that God strike her down and humble her.

Gradually, I began to hear the word God whispered to me over my tirade: forgive her. At first, I refused to pay attention.

But the mind-word became louder, more urgent—*forgive*.

Surely not, Lord! How can You ask me to forgive her when she is the offender? I sensed His response: *She is My child, too. Just as you hurt, she hurts. Forgive.*

For weeks, I stubbornly refused. Why should I forgive her when she never asked for forgiveness? I argued with God that He was mistaken to request this of me. Yet the voice persisted in urging me to forgive. Finally one day, desperate and weary of my load of anger, I cried out to God, *Why? Why should I forgive?* In a whisper of that still, small voice the reply came, *Because I forgive you. Because I loved you and the world so much, I gave Myself so that you might be forgiven.* I melted before the Sinless One, asked Him to forgive me, and then I forgave her. Peace flooded my body like a cleansing stream. All the anger washed away as I realized the power of the gift—salvation and forgiveness—both freely given.

The path to a restored relationship with my mother-in-law was crooked. We had our ups and downs, but the reminder of our mutual pain and God's gift of forgiveness made the journey possible. Today I can greet her with a hug, a smile, and an "I love you," without a hint of pretense in any of them. And all of our progress is possible because of the gift of forgiveness. ✸

For if you forgive men their trespasses,
your heavenly Father will also forgive you.
But if you do not forgive men their trespasses,
neither will your Father forgive your trespasses.

MATTHEW 6:14-15

*There is nothing we can do
to make God love us more,
there is nothing we can do
to make God love us less.*

PHILIP YANCEY

Grace Givers See Others
the Same Way God Does

Accept one another, then, just as Christ accepted you,
in order to bring praise to God.

ROMANS 15:7 NIV

Grace is as infinite and transcendent as the God from whom it flows. He is, I have found, "the God of all grace" (1 Peter 5:10), and He is abounding with mercy for the merciless, help for the helpless, redemption for anyone and everyone. There's no limit to the throng of guests invited to dine at the Master's overflowing table.

Grace is the bridge over a chasm that seemed infinite—the canyon between our depravity and His holiness. That bridge is wide and sturdy and sure, beckoning us to cross over into a life too wonderful for us to imagine.

A moment of grace can change a lifetime. In fact, a moment of grace can change an eternity.

*I have found the paradox
that if I love until it hurts,
then there is no hurt,
but only more love.*

MOTHER THERESA

Giving Brings Healing

SHARON GIBSON

"You want to do what? For who? You have got to be kidding!" I shook my head in shock and disbelief.

"Yes, honey," I heard Stan's determined voice on the other end of the phone. "They're asking if I'll take the directorship of a ranch for men. And I think I want to do it."

I gasped for breath. "Are you sure?" I couldn't imagine moving from our middle-class suburb to work with men from one of the worst slum areas of Los Angeles, known as Skid Row L.A., where my husband had been ministering.

We lived in Colorado Springs and ran two inspirational gift shops. Every day, I came to our stores with a sense of purpose and joy. The two stores prospered.

But after eight years of success, the economic ravages plaguing lots of oil-based economies crept up and stole our prosperity, our security, and my health. Our sales plummeted because so many people had lost their jobs. With crushed spirits, we struggled to pay our bills. My body crashed, throwing me into an upheaval of constant flu-like symptoms diagnosed as chronic fatigue syndrome. Slogging through the exhaustion and muscle aches, I dragged myself to work every day, clenching with white knuckles to our vision of sharing God's love through our business.

After six months of rapidly decreasing sales, my husband gave up on recovering the stores. The crisis plunged Stan into a season of intense soul searching, and one day in church, he felt called to take steps to fulfill a longtime desire to help the poor.

Then he received a call from his friend John inviting him to visit California. While Stan was there, John introduced him to the Union Rescue Mission and the opportunity to be the director of Green Oak Ranch, a satellite rehabilitation program near San Diego.

The mission selected forty hardcore addicts from Skid Row L.A. to live on the ranch, removing them from the temptations they faced in Los Angeles. The recovery program combined a twelve-step program, Bible studies, and counseling with help in reading skills and job training. During their stay, the men worked at the ranch and learned new job skills.

As Stan considered the opportunity, he sensed this mission was for him. I was terrified. I thought I knew what kind of men lived on skid row. I felt unprepared to deal with this kind of challenge. But despite my protests, he went out to California. We had closed one store, and I stayed for four months to sell the other.

After selling the second store, I reluctantly joined my husband. The first time he introduced me to the men in the communal dinning room, I felt completely lost and out of place. I smiled stiffly, and when I shook hands with the men, it was like it was happening in slow motion.

But after a few days, the boundaries and accountability at the ranch eased my fears, and I started talking with them. I hadn't realized that I'd been carrying around harsh stereotypes about them, attitudes that changed as I got to know them. I met former professionals and businessmen ensnared by addiction. An engineer, a salesman, and a mid-level government worker had all been entrapped by cocaine's highs and, now, gut-wrenching lows.

A tough L.A. gang leader, well trained in the street ways of intimidation and manipulation, had a tender side. When he was sober and content, his smile and laughter filled the hearts of those around him. Even the "bums" had stories to tell, stories that helped me understand their behavior better. One man, stricken with grief over the death of his wife and six-year-old daughter, started drinking. After twenty years, he learned to express his feelings of grief instead of escaping his pain through alcohol.

I gradually changed my mind about these men. I realized

that what they needed was a healthy, loving environment. The ranch provided a place to heal, to be challenged, to be loved. We gave what we had of our knowledge, support, and counsel to provide these men with strength—the strength they needed to make positive changes in their lives.

The staff, volunteers, and the men ate each meal together in a communal dining room. Over wonderfully cooked meals, I listened to the men talk about their failures and wounds from childhood abuse and neglect. Soon I saw each man as a treasure hidden from society by the dirt and grime of crime and addiction. Each one possessed unique and delightful gifts to contribute to the world. We expressed our faith in them and our belief in their potential to make better choices, and I joyfully watched their hardened hearts soften as we helped them process their grief and taught them new ways to think and behave.

As they shared their hearts and love with me and as I watched them heal, I also experienced healing. They were honest and open as they talked about their pain, which gave me permission to be real and talk about my feelings of loss and pain. I witnessed God's mercy toward the men expressed through us, and I began to have a greater understanding of His mercy to me. Over time, this revelation began to sink in, healing my emotions—and my physical health. Before long, my symptoms had almost completely disappeared.

I came to these men fearing them. Then my fear turned to compassion and hope that I could somehow help heal them. And in the end, they healed me. ✿

Therefore comfort each other
and edify one another,
just as you also are doing.

1 THESSALONIANS 5:11

*Kindness has converted
more sinners than zeal,
eloquence, or learning.*

FREDERICK W. FÀBER

Itty-Bitty Woman

CANDY ARRINGTON

Allene Bennett was an unlikely candidate for a teaching position at the alternative school. Standing just four-foot-ten, she wasn't exactly intimidating; and she hardly seemed a commanding enough presence to control and teach a classroom of problem students. However, her short stature paled to insignificance in proportion to her huge capacity to love. Plus, she had a God-given ability to see deep within her students' hearts and meet their silent needs, a gift she utilized to the fullest.

Early in her teaching career, her abilities were called into question. One of her first students—a tobacco-chewing, too-old-for-his-grade ruffian—towered over her and offered a critical assessment.

"Is you a girl or a woman?" he challenged and soon set out to test her assertion that she was indeed a woman.

"He would come up behind me, pick me up, turn me over, and hang me by my heels, headfirst, over the stairwell," Allene recounted. "I knew he was testing me, but I didn't back down. I was willing to do anything to reach these students."

Gradually, her spunk and courage earned their respect and gained her the title "Itty-Bitty Woman."

After several years at the alternative school, Allene met Polly. It wasn't long before she knew Polly would be her most challenging student yet. Arms folded tightly across a stained, too-small shirt, Polly marched into the classroom, headed for a seat in a far back corner of the room, and flung herself into the chair. Slouching as low as she could go without falling out of the chair, Polly casually began to draw on the desktop. Her greasy, tangled hair slanted across an unwashed face, and her hard slash of a mouth mirrored a lifetime of hurts and unmet needs. Allene saw the pain behind the sullen expression and recognized the avoidance of eye contact as a defense mechanism. Polly was definitely going to be a challenge.

Later in the day, Allene called on Polly. "Polly, please sit up in your chair and give us the answer to number seven."

"I dunno," Polly answered without adjusting her position.

Allene let it pass and moved on to another student.

At the end of the day, Allene saw Polly slide by her desk and deposit something on one corner. After all the students had gone, Allene opened the ill-folded wad of notebook paper and read the smudged words written in cramped, all but illegible handwriting—"I hate you!"

The words stabbed her heart as deeply as a knife blade. Slowly, she took a clean white piece of unlined paper from her bottom drawer and wrote three words across it: "I love you." Allene carefully folded the paper, wrote "Polly" on the outside, and deposited it in Polly's desk. She paused to place her hand on the desk and prayed a silent prayer for wisdom in reaching her troubled student.

And so, a pattern was established. Each day, Polly deposited the "I hate you" note on her teacher's desk; and each day, Allene responded with an "I love you" note for Polly and a prayer. Sometimes she included a piece of gum, a quarter, or colorful stickers with the "I love you" notes. Occasionally, Allene thought she detected a nearly imperceptible softening in Polly, but always the hope was dashed with the "I hate you" note left on her desk at the end of the day.

Gradually, Allene began adding short Scriptures to her notes to Polly. One day, with an accusatory voice, Polly asked, "Why do you love me?" With this opening, Allene began sharing tiny nuggets of truth from God's Word. But she never saw any evidence that these seeds fell on anything other than hard, barren ground.

As the year advanced, Polly sometimes achieved an academic victory. Her teacher made the most of it, lavishing her with praise and encouragement. But still the notes of hatred continued.

On the last day of school, Polly left with the other students. Disappointment swept over Allene. What had she expected? A hug? A word of thanks? She received neither, and as she returned to her desk, she was overcome with despair for there on the corner was a Polly note. Couldn't she get by just this last day without the note of hatred?

Allene's hand trembled slightly as she reached for the note. This one looked different. Instead of the rumpled notebook paper, pale pink stationery met her touch. Carefully lettered on the outside was "Mrs. Bennett." In the bottom right corner, Polly had drawn a bright purple flower with a chartreuse stem. Allene's heart beat faster as she opened the paper. Inside, written in bold magenta marker, were four simple words that melted her heart: "I love you, too."

Itty-Bitty Woman had made a big difference. ✪

*By this all will know that
you are My disciples, if you
have love for one another.*

JOHN 13:35

Faith is believing He,
the miracle worker,
can turn my stone-cold
indifference into
a fire of love toward
certain "unlovables."

PAMELA REEVE

My Friend Rose

JANET SEEVER

When I arrived at six a.m. in the large hospital kitchen, Rose was already checking name tags on the trays against the patient roster. Stainless steel shelves held rows of breakfast trays that we would soon be serving.

I gulped. "Hi, I'm Janet." I tried to sound cheerful, although I already knew Rose's reputation for being impossible to work with. "I'm scheduled to work with you this week."

A stocky middle-aged woman with graying hair, Rose stopped what she was doing and peered over the reading glasses perched on her nose. I could tell from her sour expression she was not pleased to see a student worker.

"What do you want me to do? Start the coffee?" I was feeling less confident by the minute.

Rose sullenly nodded and went back to checking name tags.

I had filled the forty-cup pot with cold water and started making the coffee when Rose gruffly snapped, "That's not the way to make coffee." She stepped in and took over.

Nothing I did pleased her after that. All morning, her eagle eyes missed nothing and her sharp words stung. She literally trailed me around the kitchen, pointing out what I'd done wrong.

Later, after breakfast had been served and the dishes had been washed, I set up my share of trays for the next meal. Then I busied myself cleaning the sink. Certainly Rose couldn't criticize the way I did that.

When I turned around, there stood Rose, rearranging all of the trays I had just set up.

Later, at break time, some of the older full-time workers decided to have some fun and started teasing me. "Are you having a good time working with Rose?" Margaret's mischievous blue eyes twinkled as she baited me with her questions. I found myself actually biting my lip to keep from crying.

Totally exhausted, I trudged the six blocks home from the University of Minnesota Hospital late that June afternoon. As a third-year university student working my way through school, I had never before encountered anyone like Rose.

With muscles still tense, I wrestled with my dilemma alone in my room. "Lord, what do You want me to do? I can't take much more of Rose."

I turned the possibilities over in my mind. Should I see if my supervisor would switch me to work with someone else? Scheduling was fairly flexible. On the other hand, I didn't want to be a quitter. I knew my coworkers were watching to see what I would do.

And as I prayed, I knew: Rose needed love. God wanted me to show her His love.

Love her? How? I could tolerate her, maybe, but with her harsh, critical words, loving her was impossible, I was sure.

"Lord, I can't love Rose. She's impossible. You'll have to do it through me."

Working with Rose the next morning, I ignored the barbs thrown in my direction and did things her way as much as possible to avoid friction. As I worked, I silently began to surround Rose with a warm blanket of prayers. "Lord, help me love Rose. Lord, bless Rose."

Over the next few days, something amazing began to happen. As I prayed for this irritating woman, my focus shifted from what she was doing to me, and I started seeing Rose as the hurting person she was—someone God loved just like He loved me.

I was the one who changed first, not Rose. As the icy tension began to melt away, Rose criticized less and less.

Throughout the rest of the summer, we had numerous opportunities to work together. Each time, she seemed genuinely happy to see me.

"I saw on the schedule they've got the two of us working

together next week," she would say as we passed in the hospital hallway. "I'm glad about that."

As I worked with this lonely woman, I listened to her—something few other people had done.

I learned that she was burdened by elderly parents who needed her care, her own health problems, and an alcoholic husband she was thinking of leaving. There was no question that her lot in life was difficult, and I began to understand what made her the way she was. I even had an opportunity to tell her that when I had problems, the Lord was my source of strength.

The days slipped by quickly as I finished the last several weeks of my summer job. Leaves were starting to turn yellow and red, and there was a cool crispness in the air. I soon would become a full-time university student once again.

One day, while I was working alone in one of the hospital kitchens, Rose entered the room. Instead of her blue uniform, she was wearing street clothes.

I looked at her in surprise. "Aren't you working today?"

"I got another job and won't be working here no more," she said as she walked over and gave me a quick hug. "I just came to say goodbye." Then she turned abruptly and walked out the door.

Although I never saw Rose again, I still remember her vividly even though forty summers have come and gone since then. In that time, I've met a lot of people like Rose: irritating, demanding, unlovable—yet hurting inside. I've learned that God loves them, and that what they need most is God's love. And even though it's sometimes difficult, it's always worth the effort to pass along the love He's given me. ✿

Love is patient,
love is kind.
It does not envy,
it does not boast,
it is not proud.
It always protects,
always trusts,
always hopes,
always perseveres.

1 CORINTHIANS 13:4, 7 NIV

> *It is the duty of every Christian*
> *to be Christ to his neighbor.*
>
> MARTIN LUTHER

Dinner with Sinners

TONYA RUIZ

I was busy with my quiet suburban life and perfect family: one husband, four children, two frogs, and an aquarium full of assorted fish. Although I home schooled the children, the aquatic animals were on their own. Tomatoes and cucumbers grew in our vegetable garden, and I received many compliments on the Calalillies blooming in the front yard. When the holidays rolled around, our Christmas gifts and cards were homemade. I cut coupons, wore flower-print dresses, cooked pot roast, and scrubbed my house spotless on a weekly basis. The Stepford Wives had nothing on me.

When new neighbors moved in across the street, I immediately decided that we had nothing in common. We had different lives, different values, and came from different worlds. Other than a hello and a handshake, I stayed away. I jokingly told myself I was way over quota on friends and neighbors anyway. There was no welcome party from me, not even a friendly plate of chocolate chip cookies. Nothing.

After playing with their kids, my son came home and told me that our new neighbors were planning their wedding. "Oh, my, they're not even married?" I asked. Rolling my eyes, I said to my friend from down the street, "My kids definitely won't be playing at their house."

Hard rock music blared from across the street at their wedding reception. "What has happened to our neighborhood?" I asked my husband as I spied out my bedroom blinds. He shook his head and said, "You look like Gladys Kravitz—all you need are binoculars."

"You're right," I said as I rifled through a drawer looking for mine.

The craziness continued until months later when my doorbell rang and there stood my nearly-new neighbor. With a desperate look on her face, she asked, "We're having some family problems; do you know of a church we could go to?" I was surprised and ashamed as I stood in a puddle of my self-righteousness.

In all my months of condemning and judging, never once did I consider reaching out to them or having them over for dinner. An invitation to church was the furthest thing from my mind. How had it completely slipped my memory that before I was a Christian, I had cohabitated with my boyfriends, listened to hard music, and gone to more than my share of parties? What if my friends had said, "We can't take you to our church concert because of your colorful language, overdone makeup and suggestive clothing"?

I was ashamed of myself. Jesus did not consider himself better than the tax collectors, prostitutes, or other sinners, why had I?

Not only did our new neighbors go to our church, but during that year they both accepted the Lord there. We have since moved across the street and bought the house directly next door to them. We have laughed together and cried together. They have become our cherished friends; only a block wall separates our lives.

My neighbors taught me something. In order to share God's grace with them, I had to see past the beer cans to their hearts and hear their desperate cries over the loud music—the way the Lord did.

My neighbors have blessed me far more than I blessed them. Because of them, my vision and hearing have been permanently improved—I'm much quicker to ask the Lord for His perspective, His hand of grace. And I have put away my binoculars. ✲

Now it happened, as Jesus sat at the table in the house, that behold, many tax collectors and sinners came and sat down with Him and His disciples.

MATTHEW 9:10

*Trying to do the Lord's work
in your own strength is the
most confusing, exhausting,
and tedious of all work.
But when you are filled
with the Holy Spirit,
then the ministry of Jesus
just flows out of you.*

CORRIE TEN BOOM

Grace Givers Give from the Heart and Lay Down Their Lives for Others

And walk in love, as Christ also has loved us and given Himself for us, an offering and a sacrifice to God for a sweet-smelling aroma.

EPHESIANS 5:2

We must understand grace, at least within the limits of our comprehension; we must understand mercy. And we must be clear on how the two ideas intersect.

Think of it this way: Mercy is God withholding the punishment we rightfully deserve. Grace is God not only withholding that punishment but offering the most precious of gifts instead.

We have seen over and over again that God, the great Grace Giver, lavishes us with blessings, meeting our needs and then some. Grace goes the extra mile; grace givers follow the Lord in laying down their lives for others.

No matter how little you have,
you can always give some of it away.

CATHERINE MARSHALL

Tied with Love

JANICE YOUNG

*E*ach Sunday morning, a group of my friends and I lead praise and worship at the DayCenter for the Homeless in Tulsa, Oklahoma. The DayCenter provides a place for struggling people to safely spend the day, with access to shower and restroom facilities, counseling services, and medical assistance.

Lots of churches send buses to pick up DayCenter clients for Sunday morning services. But some folks would prefer not to leave the center, and after a while it dawned on some of us volunteers that we could provide a worship service for them right there at the site. So each Sunday, we bring our instruments and sing songs of praise with the DayCenter residents. It's nothing fancy, but we love our simple time of worship.

In the few years we've been doing it, we've seen people come and go as they work to pull themselves out of the pit of homelessness. But Nancy is one of the chronically homeless. She's very quie, and you wouldn't know it unless you talked to her for a while, but she struggles with a mental illness that limits her ability to support and take care of herself. Because of the illness, she's been homeless on and off, and along the way she became a regular at our services. I guess I didn't realize how much the worship meant to her until recently.

This spring, something happened in Nancy's heart that made her want to give something, anything, to the Lord and to people who need help, even though she had very little to give. And so, a few weeks before Easter, she shyly approached me. She handed me a plastic grocery bag full of lavender fabric.

"What is this?" I asked her.

"This is just...my gift," she said. "My offering."

Curious, I pulled open the bag to reveal an armload of neckties printed with stripes and Easter eggs. Nancy doesn't have a sewing machine, so each of the forty ties was exquisitely handcrafted, each stitch lovingly and painstakingly sewn by hand.

I didn't know what to say or do. She just wanted to give—how could I help her neckties make a difference?

I had an idea. The next week, I took the ties to my Sunday school class at church and asked my classmates if they'd like to help Nancy's offering go further for God's ministry at the DayCenter. For whatever amount God laid on their hearts, I announced, each of the men could have a custom-made Nancy tie for Easter.

By the end of the class, we had over five hundred dollars.

When I told Nancy about how her generosity, together with the generosity of my classmates, would help people at the DayCenter, she was overwhelmed and touched beyond words. Since then, we've made plans to use part of the proceeds to buy more fabric so that Nancy can make more necktie offerings.

That beautiful, sunny Easter Sunday, all the guys in our little DayCenter worship band wore their lavender, egg-sprigged neckties, a testimony to the power of giving and sharing God's heart for the poor. ✿

So He called His disciples to Himself and said to them,
"Assuredly, I say to you that this poor widow has put in
more than all those who have given to the treasury;
for they all put in out of their abundance,
but she out of her poverty put in all
that she had, her whole livelihood.

MARK 12:43-44

God uses people to perform His work.
He does not send angels.
Angels weep over it,
but God does not use angels
to accomplish His purposes.
He uses burdened, broken-hearted,
weeping men and women.

DAVID WILKERSON

Mr. Bone's Eye

JESSICA INMAN

*S*ometimes when God uses someone as a channel of grace, He uses everything that person has, their strengths as well as what might be perceived as weaknesses. When thirteen-year-old Daniel Birkhead met forty-five-year-old Jonathan Bone, it was like everything in his life had prepared him to share God's grace with Jonathan.

The two first met at a Christmas party at the Nashville Rescue Mission. Jonathan had just graduated from a six-month program at the mission, designed to help people get off the street, and Daniel and his father and brother had drawn his name out of a hat. They bought him the Dallas Cowboys jacket he'd requested for Christmas and were going to present it to him at the party.

The dining hall at the mission was full of people, and Daniel wondered which one was "his." When they were introduced, Daniel couldn't help but think that Jonathan wasn't what he had expected. He was six-foot-four with muscular arms and legs, and he looked like he might coach Daniel's football team. But he did have one very different thing about his appearance: He wore an eye patch.

Jonathan thanked them enthusiastically when he opened his gift, but then he circled back around through the festivities to thank them several more times. And as the four got to talking, something about the family made Jonathan comfortable enough to share his story—how he'd gotten off drugs and now had a job at a restaurant, how his father had abandoned his family, how his brother died. He also told them about how when he was seventeen, he was at a football game that turned into a riot, and a gang member hit him in the face with a lead pipe, knocking out his eye. That's why he needed the eye patch.

They kept talking, but Daniel had a hard time getting past Jonathan's eye. It made him sad—Jonathan had missed out on a lot of things in life because of his eye, and kids on the bus even teased him for it. And even though Jonathan didn't say so, Daniel wondered if the eye patch made him self-conscious about looking for work. Glass eyes cost $700, Jonathan said. It was money he just didn't have.

As he and his family left the mission, Daniel couldn't stop thinking about the $200 he had in savings. *It wouldn't hurt me at all to give the money*, he thought, *but it would make Jonathan's life a whole lot better*. He told his dad what he wanted to do, and together the two of them came up with a plan to raise the rest of the money. Daniel came home, found a jar, and labeled it, "Mr. Bone's Eye" in black marker.

Not too many people would go the extra mile like that. What made Daniel so compassionate, so quick to look out for someone else?

For one thing, Daniel knows how it feels to be different. Born with a cleft lip and palate, he's endured surgeries since he was just a baby, and has had to learn to live with a slight deformity. Daniel and Jonathan connected immediately, and it was Daniel's compassion and understanding that made Jonathan so quick to share his life with the Birkhead family.

Daniel's life, like Jonathan's, hasn't been easy. He faces challenges every day, including ongoing surgeries and pain. His mom, Mary Grace, sometimes gets upset because Daniel has always gotten the short end of the stick. Lots of things just don't come easy for him. But "he's very dauntless—he knows he's going to have to work hard," she says. And part of what makes Daniel so loving is that kind of perseverance.

The hurdles Daniel faces have given him a trust in God to make him what He wants him to be, a strong determination to overcome challenges, and an incredibly tender heart toward people who feel like they don't quite fit—which made him a perfect candidate to share God's love with Jonathan in a practical, persistent display of grace.

Daniel made phone call after phone call to aunts and uncles and members of his church, asking them to donate to the fund. He left messages and waited for responses. The jar sat next to the dinner table for the next few weeks, getting fuller and fuller.

Meanwhile, even though they hadn't made contact since the Christmas party, Jonathan couldn't stop thinking about the Birkheads, and he hoped that somehow they'd get to see each other again. So he was thrilled when Rob, Daniel's dad, called to let him know they'd raised enough money for him to get a new eye.

The surgery was arranged for a couple weeks later, and Daniel and Jonathan kept in touch. The Birkheads even started picking Jonathan up for church each Sunday. When Jonathan had his new eye, he called Daniel right away—he couldn't wait to say thank you.

In the weeks that followed, Jonathan's life changed dramatically. His self-consciousness was gone, and he even landed a second job working for a newspaper. Every time he looks in the mirror, he's reminded of how far God has brought him. The eye is a daily motivator and reminder of God's mercy. He's never been happier.

Today, the Birkheads are praying with Jonathan about what's next for his life—as Rob put it, "We want to be his cheerleaders."

The future is bright for Jonathan, and for the teen whose compassionate heart God used to change Jonathan's life. ✪

I will bring the blind
by a way they did not know;
I will lead them in paths
they have not known.
I will make darkness light
before them, And
crooked places straight.

ISAIAH 42:16

We make a living by what we get,
but we make a life by what we give.

WINSTON CHURCHILL

A Dream Come True

OSEOLA MCCARTY

I began washing clothes when I was just a little girl, helping my mother and grandmother. When I started going to school, I would wash my own clothes on Saturday mornings, standing on a wooden box so I could reach the pot of water we used. In the evening, I would heat up Mama's heavy old iron on the cookstove and do my ironing. All my clothes were ready for the next week by the time I went to bed on Saturday night.

When I was about ten years old, my favorite teacher, Mrs. White, said to me one day, "Oseola, come up here to my desk." She talked to me in a low whisper so nobody else could hear: "Oseola, who irons your clothes?"

"I do."

"You do? Oh, my. Well, I've got a linen dress I'd like you to iron. What do you charge?"

"Ten cents," I replied. But when I returned the dress, freshly washed and ironed, she paid me a quarter. As time went on, one person told another about my washing and ironing, and the work just seemed to come. The more I did, the more money I made.

When I was twelve, my aunt took sick, so I had to drop out of the sixth grade to look after her. The next year my classmates had moved on; and because I had fallen so far behind, I never went back to school. Instead, I kept washing and ironing and tucking money under the pink lining of my doll buggy.

One day I put my money—maybe five dollars—in a checking account, and every month I dropped off more coins at the bank. All, that is, except for what I put in the collection plate at the Friendship Baptist Church. Nobody had taught me to do that. It just seemed the right thing to do to give God back something of what He had given me.

The years passed. I made a rule that I would always keep up my church giving, and once a year I made a payment on my insurance and on my burial plot. Every month, I paid my water and electricity and gas bills and set aside a certain amount for groceries and everyday needs. As time went on, God taught me to spend money on the things I needed and to save the rest.

One day when I went to the bank to deposit my money, the teller said, "Oseola, if you put your money in a savings account, you'll get some interest on that money."

"Yes, ma'am. When can I do it?" I asked.

"You can do it now." And I did.

Then on another visit, one of the people at the bank said to me, "Oseola, you ought to put your money in CDs and build up more money."

And I said, "Yes, ma'am. When can I do that?"

And she said, "Right now." So I did, and my money just kept on building.

When I got my license as a hairdresser, for about fourteen years I washed and fixed people's hair. But when Mama got sick with cancer, I went back to washing and ironing at home so I could take care of her.

My Mama died in 1964, and in 1967, my aunt passed on. I kept right on working, even after the age most people retire. When a touch of creeping arthritis became too much pain for me to keep working, I was mighty distressed that I had to quit work at the age of eighty-six. But I said, "Lord, I want You to stay by me and guide me and protect me in all things." And He sure did.

At the bank one day they asked me where I wanted my money to go when I passed on. Mr. Paul Laughlin—one of the officers there—sat down with me and spread out ten dimes on the desk. He told me that each dime represented 10 percent of my money. So I took a dime for the church and a dime for each cousin. That left six dimes for a dream I had always had.

"I want to help some child go to college," I said. "I'm going to give the rest of my money to the University of Southern Mississippi so deserving children can get a good education. I want to help African-American children who are eager for learning like I was, but whose families can't afford to send them to school."

Mr. Paul looked at me funny and said, "Miss Oseola, that means you'll be giving the school a hundred and fifty thousand dollars."

One hundred and fifty thousand dollars! I had never realized how much I had, and the amount about took my breath away. A lawyer whose washing I'd always done talked to me to make sure I still really wanted to follow through with my plan. Then we drew up the papers. He made sure I would still have enough money if I ever needed it, and the rest would be given out over the years ahead, year by year.

When the news of what I had done got out, folks from newspapers and magazines came round to find out who I was. I didn't see what the fuss was about, but invitations started arriving—to come visit the President in Washington, D.C., and the United Nations in New York City.

But of all the new people I met, the one who meant the most to me showed up right in my own front yard. That August, a lovely young girl ran up and threw her arms around me. "Thank you, Miss McCarty," she said, "for helping me go to college."

It was a bright girl named Stephanie, who was about to begin her freshman year. She was the first to receive a one-thousand-dollar Oseola McCarty Scholarship. Stephanie had brought along her mother, a schoolteacher, and her grandmother, who worked as a seamstress, and her twin brother, who was entering college also—and we all sat visiting on the screened-in front porch. Right off, we felt like family.

Stephanie had wanted with all her heart to go to USM, but since her twin brother was starting his freshman year as well, money was pretty tight. Even though her grades were good and she had been president of the student body at Hattiesburg High, she kept missing out on scholarships. Nonetheless, she had gone ahead and applied to USM on faith, and her family had asked the Lord for help.

"Lord, You've told us that if we asked, we would receive," Stephanie had prayed, "so I'm asking for Your help." Then she received a phone call telling her she would be the first person to receive an Oseola McCarty Scholarship.

I'm so proud. I told Stephanie right away that I'm planning to be there for her graduation. Now I feel like I've got a granddaughter.

I'm always surprised when people ask me, "Miss McCarty, why didn't you spend that money on yourself?" I just smiled.

Thanks to the good Lord, I am spending it on myself. ✿

He who gathers money little by little makes it grow.

PROVERBS 13:11 NIV

*The heart benevolent
and kind most resembles God.*

ROBERT BURNS

Green Ink

LAURA L. SMITH

*T*he rush of Christmas was again upon me. I was opening a stack of Christmas cards, glancing quickly at photos of friends' children while listening to my four-year-old daughter rehearse "The Little Drummer Boy" for her preschool Christmas program. My mind swirled with commitments, cookie recipes, and carols—and then it froze.

Staring at the letter in my hand, I couldn't draw oxygen from the air. My ears and cheeks burned as if I had just come out of the December cold into a heated house.

There was no Christmas card in the envelope. Instead, I held a letter signed by her four children, letting me know of the unfortunate passing of their beloved mother, a precious lady named Helen Tibbals. Shaking, I dropped to my kitchen floor, tears flowing down my face for the loss of this angel. And then I smiled. Helen was in heaven where she had always belonged and from where she certainly had come.

It was forty-seven years earlier that Helen first walked into my mother's living room. Countless times, Mom had told me the story. She'd heard a knock on the door of the small house where she lived with her four siblings and mother. A slim, redheaded woman and her teenage boy stood smiling at them, and Mom watched in awe as the two strangers carried armloads of packages wrapped in red with their names written on white tags in bright green ink. They also brought a pine tree, strings of colored lights, and glass ornaments, transforming the drab room from black and white to Technicolor. My mom backed against the threadbare couch to allow her and her son room to unload Christmas into the living room.

The woman in the green silk dress introduced herself as Helen Tibbals and her somewhat awkward son as Todd Junior. She was a member of First Community Church, the same church Mom's family attended, and explained that she had taken a paper gift tag off the Christmas tree standing in the church vestibule. It had their names on it.

She was all lipstick and smiles and smelled like the department store downtown. The sharp scent of peppermint filled the air as she opened a box of candy canes and invited them to join in decorating the evergreen. All the while, she asked questions about the kids as if they were her own.

Helen herself was a Christmas gift, and over time she became a part of our family. Until my mom and her siblings graduated from high school, Helen regularly brought them school supplies, new clothes, and chocolates. She even sent them to summer camp each year. When my grandmother struggled with breast cancer, Mom said Helen would bring candy bars and magazines to the small home as if she were Grandmother's sister. When my mom, aunt, and uncles were in college, Helen wrote them faithfully, always using her signature green pen. Helen attended my grandmother's funeral, my mother's graduation from high school, and my parents' wedding.

Helen's generosity expanded to the next generation as she adopted my brother and me as grandchildren, including us in her umbrella of selfless giving. She invited us to her home each summer for a feast and a stroll around her goldfish pond. Every birthday, gifts would arrive at our house, our names gracefully scrawled across the top with a green felt-tip marker.

When my husband, Brett, came home from work, he found me still weepy as I pulled a boiling pot of pasta off the stove, laid it in the sink, and scooped up our toddler, Matt, whose hands reached to the sky while saying, "Hold, Mama, hold!"

I pointed to where the tear-spotted letter lay limp on the counter.

Brett set his keys down and scanned the note. He turned and wrapped his strong arms around my quaking body. Soon I was able to exhale and push a smile onto my streaked face.

"Honey, can you get an extra name off the Giving Tree at church this year?" I swallowed hard, and then continued. "Helen came into my mom's life by picking her name from a tree. I would like to follow her example." A tear zigzagged down my cheek, and then another.

"Of course," he smiled, and kissed me on the tip of my nose.

The next day, Brett came home and pulled two yellow pieces of paper cut in the shapes of mittens from the pocket of his parka.

"The directions said to put our name on the half of the tag still hanging on the tree so the church would know who was responsible for that gift," Brett explained while easing his briefcase off his shoulder. "I guess that way, no child will go unaccounted for."

I nodded while drying my hands on the holly-embroidered towel by the kitchen sink.

"I wrote B. Smith on this tag, our tag," he said, holding up one of the canary-colored cards.

I started to walk towards him.

"And on this mitten," my husband's turquoise eyes twinkled, "I wrote H. Tibbals—in green ink." ✿

You are generous because of your faith.
And I am praying that you will really put
your generosity to work, for in so doing
you will come to an understanding of
all the good things we can do for Christ.

PHILEMON 1:6 NLT

*The most infectiously
joyous men and women
are those who forget themselves
in thinking about others
and serving others.*

ROBERT J. MCCRACKEN

Caregiver of the Century

KATHERINE J. CRAWFORD

Last year my sister lamented, "If I'd been thinking, I would have called Oprah. Mom would have been a great candidate for her Mother's Day show. I don't know too many caregivers who are eighty-three years old and taking care of their mother."

It's true that my mom is possibly the most loving caregiver in the world, selflessly giving of her time and resources for Grandma, who needs constant care. There are several members of our family that help make decisions for Grandma—one aunt lives next door to Mom and another lives just a mile away, but both have husbands with health problems and simply aren't always able to help. And so, my mom is on deck.

The frequent phone calls between Mom and me are filled with news about what they ate together, where they went on their latest trip, and how she keeps Grandma occupied and tries to give her life color and meaning.

"Mama sat by the puzzle table today and sorted the colored puzzle pieces into piles," she said recently. Another time she talked about the nine-mile trip from her house to the ocean, where she and Grandma watched the sea lions play. "Mama didn't seem to enjoy the sea lions near as much as the elk we saw at the zoo. She likes watching those big animals better than anything."

During one phone call, Mom told me about the decorative jeweled Christmas trees a lady ordered from her. "I sketch out the tree on plywood set in a picture frame. Then I fill it in with old costume jewelry. So when I brought out a dresser drawer full of broken jewelry, Mama had a great time. She sorted all the colors into piles and put the pearls in a large bowl before she took a nap. When she got up, she said, 'What pretty jewelry. Aren't these beautiful colors?' And then she sorted them into different piles. That kept her busy for a long time."

I could see the two gray heads bent over the colorful stones while they talked over the same old memories.

Last fall I received my "Bill of Rights" from Mom. She had recycled an old manila folder into a greeting card, gluing thirty-eight typed lines across it and adding her own wisdom between the lines by hand. One printed line said, "You have the right to laugh." Mom wrote: "And laugh and laugh."

After my coworkers applauded the clever card, I called Mom. "Where did you get the Bill of Rights?"

"From a Burger King place mat. Mama cut out all the lines. She did well, don't you think?"

Sometimes I feel guilty I can't help Mom take care of my precious grandma. When I expressed this to my mom recently, she simply said, "Well, why shouldn't I take care of her? I was six years old when my mother died. Then Daddy married Mama—she was barely twenty-three when she came to our house and loved us all. I think that was much tougher for her than my situation. Mama and I have a great time."

I've saved my Bill of Rights for the days when our grandchildren visit. It's a keeper. I especially loved the line that said, "You have the right to put a paper crown on your head." Mom wrote: "And be queen for the day."

If I lived closer to Mom, I'd place a crown on her head and let her reign as Queen for the Day—or, better yet, Caregiver of the Century.

In 2 Timothy 4:7-8, Paul wrote, "I have fought the good fight, I have finished the race, I have kept the faith. Finally, there is laid up for me the crown of righteousness."

Mom isn't a saint because she takes care of Grandma's physical needs or because she prays for her and with her. And maybe her diligence isn't something that will inspire an hour-long Oprah show. But the beautiful truth about Mom's life is that the way she cares for people reflects the love of the Lord. She has taught Jesus' love to many, whether she ever wears a crown in this life or not.

Does Mom think she needs a crown? No. I'm sure if I told her I wanted to buy her a crown, she'd say, "Oh, don't spend your money. I'll make one. Mama can sort the jewels for me. We'll have a great time together."

My mom is a jewel. Crown or no crown, she's truly the caregiver of the century. ✿

I have fought the good fight,
I have finished the race,
I have kept the faith.
Finally, there is laid up for me
the crown of righteousness.

2 TIMOTHY 4:7-8

When we step out in faith
and offer all we have,
God will use it in powerful ways.
How much is enough?
Just what we have
when God is with us!

JANE DOUGLAS WHITE

A Legacy of Giving

JENNIFER LYNN CARY

I once knew a boy, a special little guy. In many ways he was like most other boys nearing their teens. He had a killer set of Legos and loved to draw airplanes and jet bombers. He was crazy over hockey and wrestling, often practicing moves on his sisters. He bent the truth every now and again, especially if it redirected trouble. He was a normal, average boy.

But he was also very special and unique. He gave his heart to Jesus when he was ten years old; and though he often acted like an everyday type of boy, he was one of a kind, fearfully and wonderfully made with a tender heart and a generous spirit.

One day, he did something very normal and average for a young teen: He took his very first babysitting job. Friends of his parents were going to check out a possible new church site for their congregation, and they asked him to come over and play some games and watch TV with their nine-year-old daughter. It took all of an hour and a half, and he walked away with five whole dollars.

Five dollars doesn't sound like much, but it ended up changing the lives of hundreds of people.

The following Sunday, his pastor issued a request for prayers for guidance for the church—whether or not they should build a new site or revamp the old or just stay put. After the service, the boy found Pastor Steve and handed over the five-dollar bill. "Whatever we end up doing, we'll need money. You can put this toward the fund."

Pastor Steve's heart was moved. Here in his hand was the first answer to his prayer. He even felt compelled to share the story with the congregation (much to the boy's embarrassment). And then, the congregation was so moved by the generosity and faith of a young giver that they pledged enough money to pay off all the debts and build a much-needed sanctuary so that everyone could worship together and the church was free to grow.

Five years and many prayers later, the congregation moved into a brand-new, beautifully designed sanctuary. But they moved in without the boy. Because in addition to his giving nature, he was special in another way. Born with cystic fibrosis, he went home to heaven when he was only fifteen. The congregation poured out prayers for healing, and then for mercy for his family as they mourned his loss.

I had also prayed for this young man to be healed. Countless tears were shed as I knelt at God's feet, begging for his life. But God said no. He had a plan far beyond that which I could see or truly understand. This boy's life on earth was short, but intensely meaningful.

At the memorial service, in the very gym where the congregation had worshipped before the sanctuary was built, the line was so long that the service was delayed for fifteen minutes. Extra chairs were set up, and still there were people who stood for over two hours to pay their respects to this teenage boy who didn't think he was anything special.

During the service, people shared words of remembrance for over an hour and a half. From five-year-olds to ninety-five-year-olds, this special boy had touched the lives of many.

Today his legacy lives on. Hundreds of people of all ages benefit each Sunday from the sacrifice he so readily gave, and all who walk into the building remember the boy and how God multiplied five dollars like loaves and fishes. But that is only part of this boy's legacy. His is also a legacy of prayer. If you pull back the carpet, you'll find prayers poured out in ink over the concrete to form a part of the foundation, as if etched in stone. It's a legacy of encouragement, a legacy of grace.

God took a normal, everyday boy and poured His heart into him so the hearts of many would be moved. And even though he has gone to his eternal home, God is still moving hearts in a building and answering prayers the boy could have only imagined. His legacy will live on, and that legacy is something I hold near and dear to my heart. His caring nature and willingness to share make me grateful to God that I had the privilege of sharing a close relationship with him, even for such a brief time. When my time comes and the Lord takes me home, I will see this boy once again. I am thankful for that assurance.

This story might sound like a movie of the week, but every single word is true. I know.

The boy's name is Ian. He is my son. ✪

"There is a lad here
who has five barley loaves
and two small fish, but what
are they among so many?"
And Jesus took the loaves,
and when He had given thanks
He distributed them to
the disciples, and the disciples
to those sitting down; and
likewise of the fish, as much
as they wanted.

JOHN 6:9, 11

*The wintry portions of my life
are those which often give birth
to a deeper understanding of
who you created me to be, O God.*

PENNY TRESSLER

A Cup of Hope

BEVERLY HILL MCKINNEY

Teacups are delicate, fragile, and easily broken. Yet with smiles and comforting words from Jackie Henry, who started a "teacup ministry" to widows after the death of her husband, teacups minister care to the bruised spirits of grieving women.

"I use the teacup as a theme because in ministering to these precious ones, I found that is all you need: a cup of tea and a listening ear," she said. "Tea illuminates a memorable moment shared between ladies. It's warm and inviting and soothing. The teacup represents thoughtfulness and a caring spirit. I wanted my ministry to be warm, inviting, caring, and uplifting."

After twenty-eight years of marriage and two children, Jackie's husband died from a lingering illness. She recalls, "It was a strange world to me. There was no manual written on how to be a widow. It was no longer 'we,' just me. Everywhere, I saw reminders of my husband—in pictures or songs or my wedding ring. I vacillated between numbness and total disbelief."

Jackie was suddenly assuming new roles in unfamiliar

territory. Things like home maintenance and repairs, dealing with the car, yard work, the upkeep of the pool, and those mounting bills seemed to consume her. "Many times I would lose a thought in mid sentence. I felt I was living in the land of limbo."

One fateful morning during her daily devotions, Jackie felt the Lord direct her to several Scriptures, including Lamentations 3:22-23: "Through the LORD's mercies we are not consumed, Because His compassions fail not. They are new every morning; Great is Your faithfulness." Inspired, she decided to give the day back to the Lord, relying on His faithfulness to get her through her grief one day at a time.

Although she felt like sitting at home and feeling sorry for herself, she decided to do some Christmas shopping. She was a little bit surprised when she found herself at a store and restaurant she seldom patronized.

While waiting to be seated at the restaurant for lunch, she struck up a conversation with the lady sitting next to her. "Immediately she began telling me about her husband leaving her for a younger woman and stated she had no desire to go on with her life," Jackie remembers. "Feeling very alone, she asked me to join her for lunch."

As the two ate, Jackie realized that the Lord had placed this stranger in her path. She shared the love of the Lord with her and asked if she could pray with her. After they prayed, the two traded phone numbers before parting.

Through that experience, Jackie realized that although she often felt alone, she wasn't really alone in life. She had the Lord to guide and comfort her—and there were many other women who could walk this road with her, who needed her encouragement and comfort as much as she needed theirs.

Suddenly, she saw widows everywhere—across the street, next door, in the next town, and in her church. And as she journeyed along in her grieving and healing, she was flooded with a desire to "passionately demonstrate the heart of God in a way that people could relate to," and she discovered that "ministering to widows is a work of caring that is close to the heart of God."

Within a few years, the Lord impressed upon her the idea to begin a ministry to widows, to let them know that they're not alone and that they still have a life and a future ahead of them.

Jackie said the Teacup Ministry aims simply to "offer a cup of hope to widows. I make the initial contact after the death of a spouse by bringing a boxed gift of a teacup with a note to welcome her to our group. I share a cup of tea and visit with her—letting her lead in the conversation. Then throughout the year, I send out 'thinking of you' cards with a teabag enclosed."

The Teacup ladies plan all kinds of special events throughout the year—a spring luncheon to simply visit and share, a Christmas brunch with gifts and a short devotional on presenting each other with the gift of time, a smile, a phone call. For Valentine's Day this year, Jackie planned a luncheon she called "Celebrating God's Love," reminding each lady that God loves her very much.

An even richer part of the Teacup Ministry is the newsletter Jackie sends out that offers timely encouragement. The newsletter also lists names and contact information, and Jackie encourages everyone to "call each other once a week or so. You never know when someone needs to hear a friendly voice."

After nine years of widowhood, God sent a wonderful man into Jackie's life. Larry, her new husband, shares with her in this new ministry, helping with the events, singing solos, and sharing from the Scriptures.

But even with new and good things happening in her life, Jackie is still in touch with the needs of those who are walking through a season of grief. She has been caught by God's compassion for widows and longs to tell them of His love.

Recently, a widow whom Jackie had invited to an event came to her and said, "Thank you for insisting that I come and give it a try. It has made a big difference in my life. No one has ever touched my life the way you have. Thanks for caring. You have helped me get through these difficult holidays. I actually find myself looking forward to the next event."

Those words made Jackie's day. She loves seeing a woman's tears turn into brave smiles. She loves knowing that she has helped deliver God's compassionate care to someone who is hurting. ✲

"Comfort, yes,
comfort My people!"
Says your God.

ISAIAH 40:1

*It is not the possession
of extraordinary gifts that
makes extraordinary
usefulness, but the
dedication of what we have
to the service of God.*

FREDERICK WILLIAM ROBERTSON

Grace Givers Experience–and Participate in–Miracles

For we are His workmanship, created in Christ Jesus
for good works, which God prepared beforehand
that we should walk in them.

EPHESIANS 2:10

Grace changes people as nothing else can do. It cleanses the sins of the past. It enables righteousness in the present. And one thing it does for certain: It constantly surprises us. For the essence of grace is surprise. There is nothing shocking about giving people exactly what they deserve. Grace subverts the rules and gives people what they *don't* deserve. It is motivated by the warmth of love rather than by cold calculation. Therefore, grace is always doing something we didn't expect.

As grace floods your life and overflows into your world, be on the lookout for the unexpected. You just might find yourself right in the middle of a miracle!

God loves and cares for us,
even to the least event
and smallest need of life.

HENRY EDWARD MANNING

The Miracle of Love and Grace

DAVID JEREMIAH

*D*oes the God of the Bible still perform miracles?
Does the Miracle Worker of Nazareth still do the
impossible? Just ask missionary Bertha Smith. During
her early days in China, she settled down in the village of
Tsining, but the only accommodation she could find was an
ox stall in a villager's barn.

The worst thing about it was the flies, which were
particularly tormenting when she tried to eat. Especially on
rainy days. House flies, horse flies, black ones and green ones,
big flies and tiny ones. They nearly drove her crazy.

One afternoon Bertha talked to the Lord about it. "I am
one of Your spoiled children," she prayed. "All my life I have
been accustomed to screened houses and clean food. Now,
I just can't eat with those flies all over my food. Down in
Egypt You had flies to come and go at Your word. You are the
same today, and You are ready to work the same way if my
situation demands it. Now please do one of two things for me:
Either take the flies away, or enable me to eat and not mind
them. You then just take care of any disease germs which they

may put into my body. Just whichever You wish to do will be good enough for me!"

According to her own testimony, from that moment, not a fly flew into the ox stall. Not for the remaining five days. Not one. Bertha was in a "no fly" zone.

But...

But, as she wrote in her autobiography, Go Home and Tell, that was not the greatest miracle that occurred during her time in Tsining. "You will agree that was a miracle," she wrote. "I can tell you one bigger than that!" And she proceeded to describe how the villagers were transformed by the power of the Cross of Jesus Christ, how they turned from idols to serve the true and living God, and how the Lord used her ministry to bring the people of Tsining to Himself.

"If those people were born of the Spirit," she wrote, "that was the greatest miracle of all earth's wonders.... Flies have no enmity against God in their nature; but when a human being realizes he is deserving of hell, admits his guilt, and willingly turns away from sin and chooses Christ as his Lord, that is a miracle!"

Has God ever given you a miracle? Has the miraculous touched your life? In Christ you have the miracle of new life, having been raised from death to life. You haven't been passed over. The Christian life is, in all its elements, supernatural; and all God's children have experienced miracles. All His children are miracles. ✿

> *Therefore, if anyone is in Christ,*
> *he is a new creation;*
> *old things have passed away;*
> *behold, all things have become new.*
>
> 2 CORINTHIANS 5:17

*Dependence upon
God makes heroes
of ordinary people
like you and me!*

BRUCE WILKINSON

A Cry for Mercy

LORETTA LEATH AS TOLD TO NANETTE THORSEN-SNIPES

When my husband, Randall, took off with a friend to play pool, I was furious. Not only was he spending money we didn't have, he belonged at home with me. But things changed that night when his so-called buddy wrapped the car around a tree and ran away, leaving Randall for dead.

When the phone rang, I figured he was calling from the pool hall to say he was running late.

But instead I heard a woman's somber, urgent voice. "Mrs. Leath, your husband has been in an accident. You need to come to the hospital. Now."

I quickly dialed my eighteen-year-old daughter, Lita, who drove me to the hospital. It was blacker than tar that night, with rain clouds blanketing the moon, and it was hard to see where the country road ended and the kudzu-covered pines began. Lita's headlights raced across an accident scene where a car had hit a tree. The car was folded like an accordion around the trunk. We couldn't stop to help. Randall was hurt—we had to get to him. We couldn't have known that that was his buddy's car.

We rushed to the emergency room, where a nurse led me back to Randall. I gawked at his mangled, swollen face. *No, that's not Randall!* my mind screamed. I felt as if I had walked into someone else's nightmare. I lifted his arm and read the wrist bracelet. It was my husband, and I was living the nightmare.

After they moved Randall to ICU, I stood at the foot of his bed, taking a long, hard look and trying to process what I was seeing. I jumped when someone lightly touched my arm. "Mrs. Leath," the doctor said, drawing in a slow breath, "he may not make it through the night."

My thoughts raced. *Why won't he make it through the night? Surely he won't die. He can't leave me.*

As though the doctor read my mind, he answered, "He's crushed every bone in his face and dislocated his shoulder. We don't know what else is broken or damaged until we can get more diagnostics completed."

For the first time, reality set in. I clapped my hand over my mouth so I wouldn't scream. I picked up Randall's hand and held it between mine. "I'm here, Randall." There was no response, only labored breathing.

The next day, doctors and nurses frantically whirled around Randall. I overheard pieces of conversation and learned that he was being wheeled to the operating room. He couldn't breathe properly because of the crushed bones in his nose and face. But the two doctors working on him couldn't anesthetize or intubate because they thought it might kill him.

Stepping quickly beside Randall's gurney on the way to the operating room, the doctor said, "We need to fly him to Johns Hopkins because they have better technology."

My throat constricted. "I-I don't have any insurance." *What about the rent? The utilities? He can't go to Johns Hopkins. We're broke.*

Time must have run out on Randall, because the head plastic surgeon met with the head anesthesiologist behind closed doors. They decided to intubate—immediately.

For twelve hours, I sat in Randall's ICU room, waiting, sick with anxiety. I wanted to pray, but I didn't even know who God was anymore. As a child, I'd long ago turned my back on Him.

While sitting alone, I absentmindedly flipped through a Bible, landing in the Psalms. Something caught my eye in Psalm 86: "Hear my prayer, O Lord; listen to my cry for mercy. In the day of my trouble I will call to you, for you will answer me." (v. 6 NIV).

God, are You there? Can You hear me? I need to pray, but I don't know how. Proper church words didn't come naturally to me, so I just prayed like God was my friend. I whispered into the silence, "Randall's a good man, Lord, and I know how much You love him, but I love him, too. Please don't take him."

Almost immediately, it was as if He wrapped His arms around me and held me close. I was no longer alone. God was there. I wasn't sure how things were going to turn out, but I knew He would be with me.

Randall lay unconscious for a full week.

During that time, I had no idea what was going to happen next or how we were going to pay our bills, but God gave me such a sense of security that I no longer fretted about how I would make it to the hospital on bald tires or how I'd find time to get groceries. I just prayed, *Save my husband.* The doctors said it would take a miracle.

Then, out of the wild blue, my daughter's boyfriend sent someone from his church to pray for Randall. The pastor came almost every day. When the church, aware of our need, offered to pay our bills for an entire month, I whispered incredulous thanks to God for answering my prayer. Those kind people continued to pay all our bills until Randall went to work months later.

Randall's boss took my car to a garage and put brand-new tires on it so I could drive to the hospital. People I'd never met brought baskets of fruit and placed dishes of food in our refrigerator. My boss at the dry cleaners bought groceries.

Talk about blind faith. That's what I had. I didn't know for sure if God existed, and if He did, if He would answer my prayers. Now, I wonder how I could ever have doubted when so many angels were standing ready to meet my needs when He called on them. Remarkably, He met every need I had.

The biggest answered prayer came when Randall finally opened his eyes and looked at me. He couldn't speak because of his injuries, but his love for me glistened in his eyes. He held out his hand, and I grasped it. I had my miracle.

And I know that all those people who took care of us were a very special part of that miracle. God had promised He would never leave nor forsake me, and He didn't. He carried me through this tragedy close to His heart by the willing hands of His servants. ❁

The Lord is near to those who have a broken heart,
And saves such as have a contrite spirit.

PSALM 34:18

Pray the largest prayers.
You cannot think a prayer so large
that God, in answering it, will not
wish you had made it larger.
Pray not for crutches, but for wings!

PHILLIPS BROOKS

A God Nearby

CHRISTY PHILLIPPE

*I*n 1987, Emory May's family moved to a small town in eastern Montana where they would be ministering to an equally small congregation. He and his wife had been in the ministry for over thirty years, and they were excited about the opportunity of serving another church.

Later that year, Emory's mother, who lives in Florida, fell and broke her neck. Emory and his wife drove from Montana to spend a week with her while she recuperated. On their journey back home, his legs began to swell, and his feet felt as if he were walking on cut glass.

When they got home, Emory immediately went to the doctor. He said, "Emory, it looks as though you ate too much fast food on the road. That stuff is filled with salt and often causes some people's legs to swell."

But the problem continued to get worse.

Emory passed out in church on a Sunday night, and his wife drove him 240 miles to a hospital in Billings, Montana. They examined him and told him he had a rare condition causing the symptoms he was experiencing. There was nothing they could do, so they sent him back home.

Someone in his church mentioned that since he was a veteran, he could go to the VA hospital in Miles City, Montana. When he visited the doctor there, he was immediately hospitalized with a malignant tumor in his left lung. It was inoperable, and they sent Emory to the VA hospital in Salt Lake City for further tests. It was his forty-ninth birthday.

"I'm sorry, Emory, but if you see another Christmas, it will be a miracle." The doctor shared the news with compassion, but unyieldingly told them the harsh truth.

A church in Salt Lake City made housing arrangements for Carol, Emory's wife, and provided her with a car. It turned out that the couple she was staying with were both nurses at the hospital, so they were privy to all of the test results—none of which were good.

When she visited Emory, Carol told him of their hospitality: "In the rush of leaving Montana, I forgot my Bible, so I asked if I could borrow one from them. They loaned me an old, well-worn Bible that belonged to the man's grandfather, a preacher." Tears poured from her eyes as she told of her prayers: "Where are You, God, and why are these things happening?"

Then she told Emory about something that she had seen him do while searching for a word from God. She placed the

Bible on its spine and let it fall open. "The Scripture leaped off the page, Emory. I read it several times: 'Am I only a God nearby,' declares the LORD, 'and not a God far away?'" (Jeremiah 23:23 NIV).

Carol told Emory that she went immediately to her knees in her attic room and asked God that His will be done. "Please, Lord, I know that You are a God nearby, and I know that You want to heal Emory. I ask You to give him back his life."

Test after test only showed the same conclusion. There were too many tumors to offer hope for survival. They covered Emory's heart and both lungs. His left lung had completely collapsed, and there was no way to do surgery. Any treatment they considered was quickly dismissed as ineffective.

Two weeks into his stay, to everyone's amazement, Emory started improving. When he had entered the hospital, he couldn't walk the length of the bed, but now he could walk almost the length of the hospital. One day, fourteen doctors walked into the room and pulled the curtain around his bed. The chief medical officer said, "Mr. May, we don't know what has happened, but your tumors are gone."

Emory's reply was quick and to the point: "Well, then, I guess God healed me!"

Emory's complete recovery did not occur overnight; it took

him several months of rest and recuperation. But in April the following year, he and his son climbed a mountain in Waterton Lakes, Alberta, and the cancer has not returned. There has seldom been a day that he has not shared the love and the power of God to heal. He experienced a miracle, one that took place through the love and prayers of his grace-giving wife, who knew that God was a God nearby. ✲

"Am I only a God nearby,"
declares the LORD,
"and not a God far away?"

JEREMIAH 23:23 NIV

*Heaven is full of
answers to prayers
for which no one
ever bothered to ask.*

BILLY GRAHAM

Answered Prayer at the Fair

CHRISTY PHILLIPPE

*T*he Minnesota State Fair is also known as the "Great Minnesota Get-Together." It's a twelve-day annual extravaganza that is synonymous with Pronto Pups, cheese curds, deep-fried candy bars, and buckets of french fries. As an eight-year employee of the annual end-of-summer rite, Sandra Snider was working for the transportation department. Her job as a courtesy driver included shuttling all kinds of people—food demonstrators, musicians, cattle judges, swine judges, and dairy princesses—in a golf cart. She also shuttled plenty of lost people. Fair-goers can easily become separated from family and friends in the large crowd. This is an event that attracts more than 1.7 million guests each year.

It was in this twenty-different-foods-on-a-stick setting where Sandra encountered the power of prayer. A friend had told her that she asks God to bring people into her life who need prayer. So during her shift at the fairgrounds one day, Sandra decided to pray for the same opportunity. She told God that she was willing to be used as a vessel in any way He desired. "Send someone to me who needs a touch from You," she prayed.

The person God chose to send her way was Ann, a somewhat rude and irritating elderly woman who had become separated from her thirty-two-year-old daughter. Ann was upset, distraught, and worried sick. The way she carried on, though, you would have thought her daughter was two instead of thirty-two. Sandra reminded her that her daughter was a mature woman. "What does it matter how old she is?" the lady barked.

Sandra was told to transport Ann to her parked car. Perhaps the daughter was waiting there or had at least left a note on the windshield as to her whereabouts. As soon as Ann climbed into the seat next to her, Sandra began to sense that the Lord wanted her to pray out loud for this lost soul and the predicament she found herself in. *Not this woman, Lord!* Sandra protested silently. *She's irritating me.* Not exactly enamored with the woman God had sent her way, Sandra brushed off the prompting from the Lord and maneuvered her golf cart through the swarming crowds.

They located Ann's car. There was no sign of her daughter and no note. *I might as well return this woman to Care and Assistance and let them deal with her,* Sandra thought. But the Lord's insistence to pray continued and intensified, and her spirit finally relented.

Sandra asked Ann if it was all right if she prayed. "I suppose so," was Ann's flat, disinterested response. Sandra pulled the golf cart over to a more secluded place and turned off the engine. She then began to pray out loud. "Father God, You tell us that we have no wisdom apart from You. We need Your wisdom today. You tell us that if we ask for Your wisdom, You will give it to us abundantly and continuously. We need Your help in reuniting Ann with her daughter. You tell us that not a sparrow falls to the ground without You knowing it. You are aware of this situation. Help Ann take hold of faith and not fear. I am confident that You will work this out because You are able. Amen!"

Ann fidgeted while Sandra prayed. *Well, a lot of good this did,* she thought. *Why couldn't God send me someone who is more agreeable?*

When Sandra returned Ann to Care and Assistance and suggested she wait there, suddenly Ann bolted out the door. Sandra had no choice but to follow her, and as she did, she was surprised to hear Ann shouting her daughter's name. The high level of relief at spotting her daughter caused Ann to fling her purse and belongings to the ground and run after her daughter. Nothing was going to encumber or delay this reunion! When Ann finally caught up with her daughter, she put her face in her hands and sobbed. Then came an exclamation that took Sandra back a few steps: "She prayed! She prayed!"

The realization of what had happened hit Sandra when the two women disappeared into the crowd, arm in arm. She sat glued to the idle golf cart, oblivious to the pressing crowds around her. Tears came to her eyes. She spiritually and emotionally processed the powerful way in which God had just answered her prayer.

Less than five minutes after she finished praying with Ann, the two women were hugging necks. They had been separated for more than four hours. The fair attendance was 111,000 that day. What were the chances of Ann bumping into her daughter at the exact moment she ran out of Care and Assistance? What were the chances of a lost mother connecting with her daughter among 4.3 million square feet of exhibit space on 320 acres of land?

Sandra wondered how this grace-filled experience would touch Ann's heart. Would it give her increased faith in a God who indeed cared? God's grace came down that day, because of a grace giver who dared to pray a prayer of faith—right in the middle of the Minnesota State Fair. ✸

*The LORD is near to all
who call upon Him,
To all who call
upon Him in truth.*

PSALM 145:18

To the true disciple, a miracle
only manifests the power and love
which are silently at work
everywhere as divinely in the gift
of daily bread as in the miraculous
multiplication of the loaves.

FREDERICK WILLIAM ROBERTSON

God's Thread

HEIDI SHELTON-JENCK

My daughter was found by a stranger on a muddy road in Western China, her umbilical cord still attached. The Child Welfare Institute phoned a local Dutch foster family to take her home and do their best to keep her alive. Months later, the foster mother would tell me that this little girl survived hours of cold abandonment only through the grace of God. They called her a miracle baby for surviving the first month.

When my husband and I embarked on our adoption journey, we were just doing what we felt God had called us to do. I certainly didn't know that our lives were about to change dramatically through a series of everyday miracles.

An ancient Chinese proverb says there are red threads connecting people who may not know each other yet. I like to think of the red threads as God's threads. Our daughter's foster family began praying for adoptive parents. Soon after that, we started the paperwork that would enable us to adopt a child from China. We were connected, yet we didn't know each other.

One day, a few months into the adoption process, I had a nagging feeling, a persistent thought, that wouldn't go away. I kept thinking I should look at profiles of available special-needs children on our adoption agency website. I wasn't sure why—we hadn't been planning to adopt a special-needs child—but I looked anyway. And there she was. Entranced, I printed the picture as soon as I saw her.

I wasn't sure how to approach my husband with the idea, and it was with a little bit of trepidation that I showed him the picture. Considering adopting this child was a huge leap of faith for us. She was not only older than what we'd always discussed, but she was missing a hand. Neither of us had any personal or professional experience with limb differences.

But we were in love, and determined to give this child a home. Even so, while finding our daughter was easy, bringing her home involved seemingly insurmountable obstacles. The timeline for payments moved up by ten months. Our paperwork had to be sped up to a frantic pace, and we experienced our share of bureaucratic snags.

There were many days when I turned the whole mess over to God and admitted that I had no more solutions. But each time I gave up, another everyday miracle occurred, bringing us closer to our daughter.

On a cold, rainy winter day, after months and months of waiting and praying, we arrived at the Miracle Hotel in Guizhou

Province—only to wait another sixteen hours to meet our daughter. Finally, she arrived. I opened the hotel room door and, when I saw her, my heart sang. She was so beautiful, with thick dark hair tumbling down to her shoulders in a mass of curls. The foster family told us our daughter had grown into a stubborn, curious, smart, and determined toddler. I felt dizzy, surprised at how much I already loved her.

God's thread connected me to my daughter, to her foster family, and now to dozens of new friends in the adoption community. Through our miracle baby, I learned that ordinary people can experience no limit of everyday miracles. ✿

May the God of peace, who through the blood
of the eternal covenant brought back from the dead
our Lord Jesus, that great Shepherd of sheep, equip
you with everything good for doing his will, and may
he work in us what is pleasing to him, through Jesus Christ,
to whom be glory for ever and ever. Amen.

HEBREWS 13:20-21 NIV

*More things are wrought by prayer
than this world dreams of.*

ALFRED, LORD TENNYSON

Miracle in Ward Seventeen

CHRISTY PHILLIPPE

*D*uring World War II, Agnes Sandford volunteered as a Grey Lady in the Red Cross, working in Tilton Army Hospital at Fort Dix, New Jersey. There, amid wounded soldiers sent home from the battlefields, she was given a two-level cart filled with cigarettes, comic books and adventure magazines, candy, cookies, and sometimes flowers or fruit. Pushing the squeaky cart in front of her, she was to cover a certain section of wards, greeting each soldier with a cheery word and offering him his choice from her wagon.

As a Christian, Agnes would silently pray for the men. On ward seventeen, she met Frederick, who lay in a private room because he was about to die. He was so gaunt and shriveled that, to Agnes, he looked like a wizened old monkey. His skin was yellow, his ribs protruded from his body, and the skin fluttered between them as he breathed. There were tubes in both nostrils and attached to both wrists, and usually there was a doctor or nurse there with him.

"You look like you're about washed up," Agnes said. (She had found that the men liked this direct, unvarnished approach.)

"Yep," he replied.

"What's the trouble?" she asked. She could see no real wounds on his body.

"Blood clots," he replied unilluminatingly.

This, she thought, should not be too difficult to heal, and she told him of the power that might help him get well. He was not interested. In fact, he shut his eyes, clearly dismissing Agnes and her offer of prayer.

"Listen," Agnes said at last, her direct tone causing him to open his eyes. "If you'll just let me try this, I promise I'll never mention the matter again, win or lose. Now how about it?"

"Okay," the man said wearily and with a definite lack of enthusiasm. But when he drew back the sheet, Agnes shrunk back in horror. His abdomen looked like a pool of dark blood, barely covered by a thin membrane.

"Guts torn out," he said, noting Agnes's dismay. "They didn't want to carry me in from the battlefield, but I told them they had to."

Frederick had been kept alive for months by intravenous feeding, drugs, and stimulants. Agnes knew that if she had seen his abdomen at first, without a stomach or any other digestive organ as far as she could see, she would not have spoken such words of faith. But it was done, and she couldn't retract it. So she bravely laid her hands on the two sides of the red, gaping pool of blood, envisioned a stomach and all other organs perfectly formed, and then called upon the Lord.

When Agnes reached home that day, she called every prayer group she knew and asked for help. And she herself prayed for a miracle to take place in Frederick. It would require an out-and-out miracle. This would be no speeding up of normal healing processes; Agnes knew that nothing could save Frederick except the direct work of God through Jesus Christ.

The next week, Agnes passed Frederick's room with fear and trembling; but he was asleep, and she did not go in. A week later, two weeks after her prayer, she again passed his room. It was empty. He was not in his bed, although the bed was rumpled, his things were scattered around, and his name was still on the door. She went on to the common room at the end of the ward where men sat about in wheelchairs, but she did not see him. Then her eyes fell upon a good-looking, ruddy-faced young man across the room. He bore not the slightest resemblance to the wizened old monkey for whom she had prayed in the room. The young man gazed at Agnes with a twinkle in his eyes and a knowing grin.

"You can't be Frederick, can you?" Agnes asked the man.

His grin broadened. "Yes, ma'am, I am," he replied.

Remembering her promise, Agnes made no reference to his healing, but simply said, "What are you going to do now?"

"I think I'll go to South America and get a job," he said.

The next week, he was not in his room. He had been discharged and was at home.

Shortly after that time, Agnes had a brief talk with a chaplain. She recounted to him the story of Frederick because she knew that he had visited in ward seventeen and must have seen the young man.

"Is that what happened to him?" the chaplain exclaimed in amazement. "As soon as he could get out of bed, he was down in my office every day. He wanted a Bible, and he wanted to know all about God and Jesus Christ."

Agnes was used as a channel of grace to bring about a miracle in Frederick's life. Because of her step of faith in praying a prayer of healing over his damaged body, she allowed herself to be a conduit of God's healing power to Frederick, both in body and spirit. ✿

And the prayer of faith will save the sick,
and the Lord will raise him up.
And if he has committed sins, he will be forgiven.
Confess your trespasses to one another,
and pray for one another, that you may be healed.
The effective, fervent prayer of
a righteous man avails much.

JAMES 5:15-16

*Satan trembles when he sees
the weakest saint upon his knees.*

WILLIAM COWPER

In Jesus' Name

CHRISTY PHILLIPPE

*I*t was a phone call no one ever wants to receive. Mike picked up the phone to hear a friend say that their mutual friend, Debbie, was dying of leukemia and was at a cancer treatment center in Seattle.

Later, Debbie's husband called, telling Mike that Debbie had slipped into a coma. The doctors had given her just two to three days to live. Debbie's two adult children had flown in to say their goodbyes. Debbie's husband invited Mike to come and pray.

This would be a huge stretch for Mike's faith. He asked a friend to go with him, and they set out for Seattle. As they drove, Scripture passages raced through Mike's mind, and he anxiously hoped he could spread faith in God's goodness in the tension of the hospital ward. How should he pray? What should he say to Debbie's friends and family? More than anything, he wanted to share God's grace and power.

At the hospital, Mike and his friend introduced themselves to Debbie's family and then approached her bed. Mike silently asked the Lord what to pray, and Luke's account of Jesus rebuking a fever came to his mind (see Luke 4:38–39).

Debbie was a sad sight. By all outward appearances, the prayer Mike was about to pray seemed entirely impossible. But he forged ahead and prayed a strong prayer for Debbie's healing.

Mike's prayer was simple, based on Scripture and spoken in faith in Jesus. Not sure what else he could offer the situation, Mike and his friend said their goodbyes.

Debbie continued to stay on Mike's mind and heart over the next few days, but he also knew that the Lord had heard his prayer. Mike placed the entire situation in the Lord's capable hands.

A week later, Mike's phone rang. It was Debbie herself. She had awoken from her coma and had asked the medical team to unhook her life support. When she heard that Mike had visited her several days before and had prayed for her, she was astonished.

"Would you please come back?" she asked.

The next day, Mike drove back to Seattle to see with his own eyes what the Lord had done.

It was an amazing visit. Debbie—alert and smiling—told an incredible story. For three days after Mike had prayed for her, while still in a coma, she sensed that an angel had been standing by her bed. On the third day, she woke up and knew in her heart that the Lord had completely healed her. The doctors' tests showed no sign of any cancer whatsoever. Her family was ecstatic.

Mike was then able to share the Gospel with Debbie's friends and family. As a result of her healing, her son and his wife received Christ and are now joyfully serving Him. And to this day, five years later, no cancer has returned.

Mike was a grace giver in the life of Debbie and her family. Because of his faith in God's power and sovereignty and his willingness to simply be there, her life was forever changed, touched with the power and grace of God. ✪

And whatever you ask in My name,
that I will do, that the Father
may be glorified in the Son.

JOHN 14:13

*I am a little pencil
in the hand of God
who is sending a
love letter to the world.*

MOTHER THERESA

Grace Givers Change the World

This same Good News that came to you is going out
all over the world. It is changing lives everywhere,
just as it changed yours that very first day you heard and
understood the truth about God's great kindness to sinners.

COLOSSIANS 1:6 NLT

Do you ever worry about your ability to serve God, to change the world for Him?

In 2 Corinthians 12:10, Paul tells us, "I take pleasure in infirmities, in reproaches, in needs, in persecutions, in distresses, for Christ's sake. For when I am weak, then I am strong." He hated the thorn that plagued him. But in time, he accepted it. He knew there could be no ministry if there was no trial because this life wasn't about Paul's strength but God's.

An ordinary person, captured by the extraordinary grace of an extraordinary God, can change the world.

Start by doing what's necessary; then do what's possible;
and suddenly you're doing the impossible.

ST. FRANCIS OF ASSISI

God is not unjust;
he will not forget
your work and the love
you have shown him as you
have helped his people
and continue to help them.

HEBREWS 6:10 NIV

You must live with people
to know their problems,
and live with God in order
to solve them.

P. T. FORSYTH

Teaching the World

KATHRYN LAY

When my husband and I began dating, I knew that his heart was to help people from around the world. I never dreamed we would teach the world together.

Nine years ago, Richard began helping two students from our local college to broaden their English skills by meeting with them one night a week. We had worked with refugees before, helping them adjust to the country and becoming their friends.

Richard's college students began telling others about this man who was helping them for free, and before long he had several students to tutor. A full-time public school teacher, he couldn't tutor during the day, so he enlisted a friend to tutor a few of the students.

More came, and more help was needed. Soon he separated the classes into two groups according to their skills and needs. That eventually became four classes: low beginners, high beginners, intermediate, and advanced. Within six years, more than a hundred students from all around the world were coming to learn or improve their English reading, writing, and cultural understanding.

Through this ministry we have named "No Longer Strangers," there have been many opportunities for the ministry volunteers to share our faith during holiday parties and in our homes. At the end of one school year, we were able to show the Jesus Film in six different languages in different rooms at our church.

A need for transportation for women who were anxious to learn English began another way of helping our students. Every Monday and Tuesday night, two or three vanloads of women and children unloaded at classes, while other men and women drove in their own cars.

Childcare was our next step to help these families. Our daughter became a part of a growing and changing group who babysat small children and helped the older ones with their homework.

As teachers, we've seen students get better jobs, feel more comfortable in meeting and making American friends, and pass their citizenship tests to become a part of the new country they love.

"My teacher, my teacher," a woman yelled one day as we walked through a department store. A young woman who had once been a student at the school ran up to us and grabbed my husband's hand.

"Oh teacher, it is so good to see you again. I tell you good news. Because of school, my English is better. I get job at school for small children and help the teacher." She smiled as if she were holding the President's hand. "It was you, Mr. Lay. You taught me good. I have good job. My husband happy. My children proud. I thank God for you."

She turned to me and grabbed my hand. "Thank you, too."

She hurried back to her family, who watched, then waved at us.

There are many times on Monday evenings when I've been tired from a day of home schooling my daughter and would prefer to stay home. Richard comes home tired from a full day of teaching junior high kids. We've complained that we'd rather stay home and rest.

But, as a family, we go to our church every Monday and begin setting up classrooms, making copies of lessons, preparing registration test materials, and making sure the other volunteer workers arrive and have the things they need to teach their students.

Our twelve-year-old daughter has helped and taught the little children since she was eight. They smile at her. When they are afraid, she calms them.

We are thankful that God has brought so many students who return and tell of us how the classes have made their lives better. And we are thankful for those who move away and cannot thank us, but we know that they have been blessed and seen the power of God's love.

A student comes into the office and I show her to her class. Other students come, their clothing different than mine, their skin darker than mine, speaking broken English with a heavy accent. But we hug one another and she finds a seat. Another lesson begins and a life is changed. ✿

*The LORD has
announced his victory
and has revealed
his righteousness
to every nation!*

PSALM 98:2 NLT

I have found that if, instead of praying for my own comfort and satisfaction, I ask the Lord to enable me to give to others, an amazing thing happens—I find my own needs wonderfully met. Refreshment comes in ways I would never have thought of, both for others, and then, incidentally, for myself.

ELISABETH ELLIOTT

One Child at a Time

DR. BELLA GENTRY AS TOLD TO LAURIE KLEIN

Among the sap-green ripple of rice in the Cambodian flood plain, along the Mekong River, the paddies are bordered by gangly sugar plums with powder puff foliage—like an illustration in a Dr. Seuss book. Packed earth roads meander along, the width of an ox cart.

Years ago, I joyfully accepted what I felt was a prompting from the Lord to serve in Cambodia as a doctor and missionary, tending to children like Pait. When I first laid eyes on little Pait, I saw a boy with dusky skin, swollen belly and legs, orangish hair, and sores all over. The floor of his house on stilts was so riddled with holes that once during the rainy season, one of his siblings fell through—and drowned.

The first time I visited Pait's tiny home, his mother was in mourning for yet another child, Pait's baby sister. Pait needed care, so I took him to stay with me for a while to tend to him. What I didn't realize was that he'd been "given" to me. I was just learning the language and customs, and I didn't understand that his mother thought I'd be keeping him permanently. Within weeks of being treated for pneumonia, worms, and beri-beri—as well as receiving ample doses of love from my family—little Pait had picked up scraps of English and was brimming with energy.

I joyfully sent him home. But ten days later he was returned, starving and listless. Pait's mother, having already lost two children, believed he'd die if left in her care. So I nursed him back to health again. Eventually, through many visits back and forth and lots of legal intervention and prayer, Pait's mother regained the confidence to raise him herself.

With wrenching challenges like these plus the needs of my own family, I came to cherish times of corporate worship, a chance to soak in grace so that I could pour it out again. I loved our church services in Sway Chroom, singing in a building perched on stilts, its floor loosely slatted with bamboo, its walls, like those of my Cambodian home, constructed from sliding panels of leaves. An ordinary church has a parking lot; we have a mound of flip-flops. More than once, I've mixed up mine with someone else's.

September days in Cambodia are sultry, with a wilting, airless heat—the kind that assaults you when you lift the lid on a bubbling kettle. It saps your energy, lays in your lungs like congealed fat. The air smells of fish and frogs and old wet mops. In those initial weeks, as we Gentrys labored among the villagers, the strain of culture shock, with its rollercoaster emotions, left us wearied and troubled, homesick some days almost beyond bearing.

In addition to homesickness, I struggled with how to help the people I met, and I relied on the Lord daily for wisdom. How does one meet needs like those of a dying mother who walked all day with her starving six-month-old son to my house for help?

When she arrived she could barely breathe. She was obviously near death from heart failure, and her abdomen was enormous. For months, she'd eaten nothing but rice and salt.

I rushed to feed and house them, grateful to see them rally. But the mother, a chronically mistreated, then deserted "second wife," escaped as soon as she could, leaving her son behind. A week later, a coworker brought her back, deathly ill again. This time, she stayed with us long enough to get well.

The poverty, the language barrier, the rough conditions— there were times I was simply overwhelmed. Sometimes I felt like Hagar, the mother of Ishmael, wondering if God really saw me. Why were there no clear victories in our labors? Worse, back home, the World Trade Center towers had just fallen, making international travel impossible. We hadn't quite despaired, but it was distressing to realize we couldn't return home.

One Sunday, I woke up to the usual racket: the local rooster brigade, all screech and strut; the freeway-like drone of a thousand insects; the saffron-robed monks chanting. Sunshine flooded the skies and rice fields. But despite the beauty around me, I was really low that morning.

I rolled off my sleeping mat and swept aside the mosquito netting. The night before, I'd pulled back the leaf panel wall to reveal the starlight, and now I blinked against acres of light and sky. My ears were bombarded with unexpected, yet familiar sounds—shrill, nasal voices, a keyboard, guitars. Someone had powered up the scratchy PA system for the Sabbath. Usually incomprehensible to my ears, today's music was different. They were playing a Khmer version of a song I knew and loved, one composed by a friend of mine: "I love You, Lord."

The lyrics swept over me, buoying my tired spirit. I knew that, like Hagar, God saw and remembered me, even halfway around the world. Faith and hope revived in my heart, and with them the courage to fight for the lives of destitute children.

Just before I returned to the States, I made sure the deserted mother and her son had entered a shelter where their basic needs would be provided along with training in a trade—

a future. Tearfully, the woman asked me to name the tiny boy. My family and I called him "Tialin Kwikulu"; in Khmer, "Tialin" means "shield," and "Kwikulu" is an African word for "faith in God."

I hoped that faith in God would indeed be their shield. I know it had been mine. ✿

Fear not, for I am with you; Be not dismayed,
for I am your God. I will strengthen you,
Yes, I will help you, I will uphold you with
My righteous right hand.

ISAIAH 41:10

*We must move from asking
God to take care of the things
that are breaking our hearts,
to praying about the things
that are breaking His heart.*

MARGARET GIBB

The Light of Love

JESSICA INMAN

When Marcia Mitchell first laid eyes on her baby daughter, Missy, she was delighted—such a perfect little girl in every way. Then, when doctors told her that Missy had a form of albinism and would be at best legally blind, they advised her to "take her home, love her, and treat her like a normal child," and she was determined to do just that.

But Marcia and her husband, Phil, were worried. Marcia knew that the first six years of a child's life are a critical learning and developmental period and that much of a child's learning is done visually. Worse, they observed signs that Missy wasn't progressing developmentally the way a baby should. How could she "treat her like a normal child" and ensure that her baby's brain would develop properly if she wasn't sure how much her baby could see?

Fortunately, Marcia found a center a little over an hour away that specialized in small children with visual and auditory disabilities. They would teach Marcia to help her child at home, and by the time Missy reached her preschool years, her parents were relieved to find that she was developmentally right on target.

But Sharmon, Missy's playmate and the daughter of their friends Pat and Sheryl, wasn't as fortunate. Because she had a motor disorder in addition to her visual impairment, the center couldn't work with Sharmon on a monthly basis the way they worked with Missy—she needed daily professional care. Pat and Sheryl couldn't move closer to the center, and there were no similar facilities in their city.

There was only one thing to do. Sheryl and Marcia went on a crusade, asking pediatricians in their area to start an early childhood program for children with disabilities. Their efforts came to a halt when one doctor told them starkly, "If you want a school like that here, you're going to have to start it yourself."

Even though those words were discouraging to hear, they came to be prophetic. Marcia and Sheryl felt determined that God was leading them to found a place where small children with disabilities could get the help they needed. By that fall, the Little Light House had opened for business in a small white frame house owned by the Recreation Center for the Physically Limited. They had one very energetic teacher, five students, and five volunteers.

Over time, they experimented and developed a curriculum and innovative teaching methods for a variety of disabilities.

Countless prayer sessions and financial miracles later, the school
is now thriving in a $2.2 million facility.

Marcia and the Little Light House directors have succeeded
in creating a school that provides a place for special children,
birth through six years of age, to develop properly. But, most
importantly, the Little Light House is a place where kids are
loved the way they are.

Marty, whose six-year-old daughter is a Little Light
House student with Down syndrome, first called the school
when Avery was only a few months old, hoping to get on
a waiting list. The first months of Avery's life had been a
trying time spent largely in the hospital, the doctors' faces
grim every time they talked about her future, and this young
mom was exhausted. When Marty told the Little Light House
receptionist that Avery might have Down syndrome, she
responded, "Oh, you are in for such a treat. They're the most
loving, sweet children."

That was the first time a non-family member had spoken
lovingly and hopefully about Avery. It gave hope to a young
mother simply to have her child treated like a person. Avery
did enroll at the Little Light House, and she's doing beautifully.
And the receptionist was right: She's a loving, engaging,
compassionate child.

When four-year-old Haley first came to the Little Light House, all her mother could think about was what her daughter would never be able to do, the experiences her disabilities would keep from her. She felt robbed of a bright future for her little girl, and she was devastated. But, she says, "The Little Light House welcomed our entire family with support, prayer, love, and laughter from the moment we walked in the door. They helped us see the joy in God's creation of life, our Haley." Haley has learned her letters, numbers, and colors, and her speech is improving rapidly and consistently, and her mom thanks the Little Light House.

Countless parents echo the same gratitude. Said one parent: "So many people treat my child like they have this condition to be treated and dealt with. But here, it's different. It's like, no, this is a *kid*." Little Light House students are kids first, kids with special needs second.

And that's what makes the Little Light House a grace-giving place. Not only are kids who might otherwise lag behind developmentally given a chance to develop the language and motor skills that give them a head start on a successful life; but they're also given a place where they are valued, where they are more than their disabilities. Here, disabled kids experience God's fierce, unconditional, unquestionable love for them—with or without disabilities.

That love is now reaching all across the globe as the Little Light House takes strides to train workers in developing countries to help children with special needs. The goal is to value and love children everywhere the way God loves them, and to help them reach their full potential. For hundreds of children, that goal has been a life-changing one. ✵

Whoever welcomes a little child
like this in my name welcomes me.

MATTHEW 18:5 NIV

*Start by doing
what's necessary;
then do what's possible;
and suddenly you're
doing the impossible.*

ST. FRANCIS OF ASSISI

Going Global

ANDREW NIMICK AS TOLD TO JESSICA INMAN

With a few stamps and a prayer, I dropped the envelopes into the mailbox, sending in the paperwork that would establish the Global Network of Independent Missions as an IRS-recognized 501(c)(3) organization. Six years ago, I never would have seen this day coming.

The idea had first come to me in very rudimentary form at a New Year's Eve party my wife, Daleen, and I attended. According to our friend Karl's tradition, each of us sat down and prayerfully wrote out goals for the new year. At that time, I'd been mulling something over. What if there was a way to give people choices for their charitable donations in the form of a portfolio-like structure similar to that offered by financial advisors? I wasn't sure just what that kind of structure should look like, but I wrote the idea down. For the time being, that's where it would stay: on paper.

As time went on, Daleen and I took a couple of mission trips overseas, including trips to India and Ecuador. More than any experience we'd ever had, those trips showed us how blessed we were. Sometimes we'd look around our house, incredulous at how much we had. God was working on our hearts, creating in us a desire to bless others out of our abundance.

We met so many wonderful people in India and Ecuador—not least of which were the indigenous missionaries serving their countries without the financial security of a large missions organization to support their outreach efforts. Their resources were often meager, and yet they worked with such joy and perseverance.

One of these precious workers was the man we came to know as Brother Henry Bhasker, who operates the Good Shepherd Mission in Puttur, India. He's always busy—Good Shepherd runs hostels for orphans and the elderly, a hospital and rural medical clinic, and twelve village churches. During her medical mission trip to India, Daleen brought back rolls and rolls of pictures of smiling orphan children. I think we were both a little overwhelmed by the need and the work that was going on.

Several years passed. And then, during a month when my church was emphasizing living with purpose, Daleen and I felt ready to take a step, to create the network I'd first envisioned six years earlier: The Global Network of Independent Missions was born.

Our first step was to create an e-mail newsletter so that people could learn more about special workers like Brother

Henry. We started out with just Good Shepherd Mission and a few e-mail addresses. Then we expanded to include updates from an organization called Hope for the Children-Nigeria in our newsletter. As we added new projects and new names to our newsletter list, we let our readers know about specific financial and prayer needs and allowed them to specify where they'd like their gifts to go.

We wanted the "network" part of the organization to help people like Brother Henry get what they needed. On one occasion, one of our contacts needed a laptop. So we found someone who was able to donate it, and someone else who was going to that country and could take the laptop on the plane with them. Another time, Samaritan's Purse assisted in funding medical clinics and HIV and AIDS education for Hope for the Children-Nigeria. We strive to utilize available resources rather than simply funneling cash to our directors.

Things just kept building and growing from there. We'd been in operation for about eight months when we learned that Good Shepherd desperately needed a new van—their dilapidated old van was held together by duct tape and Indian ingenuity. So even though $11,000 was a lot more money than we'd worked with before, we told Brother Henry we would raise the funds for their new van.

We needed the money by December 31. In early December, things were looking pretty bleak. I called Brother Henry and asked him how he would feel about only receiving half the money, but I didn't feel good about the conversation. I really wanted to give Brother Henry the whole van, but it looked like it was going to take a miracle. It was time to trust God.

We got our miracle when a large donation came in at the last minute. I've never seen a better-looking vehicle than the small maroon van Brother Henry bought with our funds. We gave God full credit for His faithfulness.

Without a doubt, the mission directors we work with make an immeasurable impact on the lives of people they touch with the love and good news of Jesus Christ. One of our favorite stories is that of Sweetie. She was found, an abandoned and abused little girl, and brought to Good Shepherd, scarred spiritually and physically. At the orphanage, she was fed and given medical attention—and loved. The picture we have of her is of a smiling face, just like all the children at the orphanage.

We love those faces—they inspire us. We know that Brother Henry and people like him need a source of support and encouragement in order to help the lost and hurting people in their communities, and that's just what we want to do for them.

Watching the ministry take shape has been a lesson in

grace for us. None of this would have happened apart from God's help and direction—it's as if He orchestrated every move we've made, and we're just grateful to be along for the ride. We're grateful for the opportunity to participate in God's work around the world. ✿

God is not unjust; he will not forget your work
and the love you have shown him as you
have helped his people and continue to help them.

HEBREWS 6:10 NIV

*When you say that
a situation or a person
is hopeless, you are slamming
the door in the face of God.*

CHARLES L. ALLEN

Where None Ever Bloomed Before

GENE BECKSTEIN AS TOLD
TO GLORIA CASSITY STARGEL

*I*t's a steamy mid-August day at the Melrose Housing Project. In the community building that we rescued from neglect, I stand among "my kids"—the diverse treasury of priceless children who live in this low-income area.

As I pass around small brown paper bags at snack time, one little fellow calls out, "Mr. B, Mr. B, come sit over here!" I pull out a pint-sized, well-scuffed white chair and silently thank the Lord that, at age seventy, I can still fold my lanky, six-foot-two frame into that little space.

I welcome a few minutes of rest. Throughout the morning we've been learning all sorts of things—things like how to tell time and how important it is to be respectful, to say "ma'am" and "sir" when talking with others—and discussing short Bible verses.

This is the fun part, this time sharing with the little ones. The remainder of each day and night it's full speed ahead as I work with all ages, trying to address their needs. And there are so many needs—from the countless cases of hunger and homelessness and drug and alcohol addiction to a simple lack of motivation, from people living with AIDS to frightened children who endure a constant barrage of family strife, we see it all.

But the most insidious problem of all—a common one among the poor—is hopelessness. An excellent example is the day I told some of the mothers that we were going to plant a flower garden. One lady said, "You'll never get flowers to grow here."

"Why not?" I inquired confidently.

"Because the kids will just tear them up," she retorted.

"Not my kids," I boasted.

I know well the hopelessness in the hearts of these people who were born into poverty. I've lived it myself. I know how that child feels who gets on the school bus without so much as a pencil, watching the other children with their shiny new lunch boxes and fancy pencil cases.

As I sit beside the children and feel the hopelessness that taunts them, I can't help wondering, *Am I planting the seed of hope in their lives? Am I giving them the mental and spiritual tools they will need to harvest that seed? How about this little fellow sitting next to me? Can I instill in him the hope of better things to come? Can one person really make a difference?* And then my mind begins to wander as I remember one person who made that difference in my life, who revealed that hope to me.

Born in the tenements of Buffalo, New York, I grew up well

acquainted with violence—it was a way of life on the streets. One night I was awakened by the thunder of gunshots. Looking out the window, I saw a man die in the street. Oddly, it didn't seem that unusual.

Our dad was a part-time prizefighter and a full-time alcoholic; between my dad and my seven brothers, we were a real "physical" family, frequently expressing ourselves with punches and shoves. I suppose it was to be expected when, at age thirteen, I beat up a guy and spent eighteen months in a training school.

Everyone I knew was into stealing—hubcaps, bikes, anything we could find, really. Most of the kids I grew up with are either in jail or dead from alcohol and drug abuse. They were like the vast majority of people born into poverty: They suffered from that terrible hopelessness and didn't know a way out.

A four-year stint in the Marine Corps opened a new door for me—for the first time, I learned that there was a life beyond the ghetto. But getting that life required education, and I had barely scraped by in high school. The GI Bill paid tuition for veterans, and that was my one-way ticket out of the slums—by way of New York University.

My life suddenly changed one fateful day in June. I was twenty-nine years old and a college student. My friend and I had taken a bus to Rochester to attend a program in church—a place foreign to me. After the singing ended, a giant Purdue football player spoke. John was six and a half feet tall and talked about knowing God. I'd never heard anyone talk about knowing God personally before.

After the program concluded, I walked up and shook John's hand. I asked, "Do you really believe all that rubbish?"

Looking me square in the eye, he answered, "I certainly do." Then he talked to me some more, explaining his faith, and for the very first time I saw that it was possible for people like me to know God. John wrapped his huge arms around my shoulders and began to pray. As he prayed, I knew I'd caught a glimpse of God. All at once I started to cry, and I prayed to accept the Lord into my life. It hasn't been the same since.

Back home in Buffalo, I found an old, inner-city church where the people accepted me just as I was. There I learned to share with others the good news of God's love. After migrating southward and serving for thirty-seven years as a public school teacher and counselor, I am retired and helping to serve the people of this community. My wife, Margie, and I sold our charming home across town and moved into a modest little house next door to the Melrose Project so that we could be more accessible to the people.

Two little grubby hands interrupt my reverie and deliver me back to the present. "Wanna bite of my bologna sandwich Mr. B.?" Thrusting the bread toward me, the donor smiles and instantly melts my heart.

"Sure," I say and take a bite. "Thanks," I add gratefully. The small owner's face lights up in a broad grin as I wrap my arm around his lean shoulders. In his eyes, I catch a glimmer of newfound self-esteem—almost as if to say, *I can make something of myself. You'll see.*

It's late afternoon as I stride along the concrete walkway that crisscrosses the housing project's postage-stamp yard. Children of all different sizes and skin tones hold my hand or skip along beside me; I must look like a long-legged pied piper.

"Let's go check out our flower garden," I suggest to the active little crewmembers that helped to plant the seeds back in the spring. The children's beaming faces tell me all I need to know. I am planting seeds of hope in their lives.

Now I'm beaming as we stoop to admire the flowers—delicate, beautiful flowers blooming where none ever bloomed before. ✦

And let us not grow weary while doing good,
for in due season we shall reap if we do not lose heart.

GALATIANS 6:9

*You who have
received so much
share it with others.
Love others the way
God has loved you,
with tendernesss.*

MOTHER TERESA

Grace Givers Are Blessed as They Bless Others

The generous soul will be made rich,
And he who waters will also be watered himself.

PROVERBS 11:25

In 2 Corinthians 9:8, Paul writes, "God is able to make all grace abound toward you, that you, always having all sufficiency in all things, may have an abundance for every good work."

Notice the repetition of the word *all*. *All* grace abounds toward us so that we are *all* sufficient in *all* things. He is all we need in all we face, so that for all we do, we can overflow with His grace and power. Did you know it was possible to live like that?

But the beauty of grace is that not only does God equip us for all things, but He also blesses us beyond our expectations. Ask anyone: When God uses us to bless others, we come away feeling more blessed than the people we tried to help.

*There is but one
way to tranquility
of mind and happiness,
and that is to account
no external things thine own,
but to commit all to God.*

EPICTETUS

Unexpected Blessings

JIM SNIPES AS TOLD TO NANETTE THORSEN-SNIPES

A few weeks after my third job layoff in six years, I stood at the stove browning hamburger while my wife worked in her office. I stepped away for a minute to go through the bills. Before I could return, Nan had rescued the burning hamburger—our last package of ground beef. In an effort to help fix dinner, I'd created a disaster.

Being laid off after twenty-six years with a company was bad, but even worse were the next two layoffs and the continual loss of salary. I wondered what would become of us.

During the first layoff, I felt discouraged. I had worked hard to get into management. In all my years there, I'd used less than ten sick days and had been a loyal employee. But I discovered that everyone was expendable.

One day, Nan interrupted my daily ritual of sending out résumés. "Jim," she said,

"I just heard on TV that Hurricane Mitch destroyed Honduras."

What did I care? Honduras was a million miles away from my busy, frantic thoughts of gaining employment.

She continued, "The people there have nothing. They only have the clothes on their backs."

I had to find a job, and she was getting on my nerves.

"I think we should give some food to the Hondurans," she began. "And we have some old clothes we can send, too."

I could feel the heat rising in my face. What? Give food to someone else? We could barely feed ourselves.

I began to argue, but stopped when she said she felt as if God was prompting her. Later that day, we took the items to a nearby church. While standing in the basement talking to the pastor, Nan whispered that we should give more. I nodded in agreement. She pulled out our checkbook and within minutes, she'd written a check for $100—money we could ill afford to spend.

I wasn't looking forward to the coming weeks of hitting the bricks. But, to my surprise and joy, because of our obedience, the job doors swung open. By stepping outside of ourselves and giving sacrificially to the "least of these," God began pouring out blessings, and I soon found a job.

Even though our season of unemployment didn't end right there, we found that God was more than faithful. One worry was our pre-existing health issues—we needed to be insured or risk losing our insurability. Interim insurance was costly, but we absolutely had to have it. One day, with my spirits flagging,

I opened my mailbox to find a letter from our church. "We have received an anonymous donation for you. The donor is praying for you and felt directed by God to help." Tears welled in my eyes. That check would pay for our insurance.

In no way did I deserve God to supply our needs. I had been an obstinate, spoiled child not wanting to part with my money, my possessions. Yet God, in His infinite, wonderful grace, supplied our needs every step of the way. And within two weeks of that unexpected check, I landed the job I have today. Just another blessing from a God who generously gives when we give to others. ✿

And God is able to make all grace abound toward you,
that you, always having all sufficiency in all things,
may have an abundance for every good work.

2 CORINTHIANS 9:8

*It is one of the most beautiful
compensations of life that
no man can sincerely try to help
another without helping himself.*

RALPH WALDO EMERSON

Hope Does Not Disappoint

MARGARET LANG

*T*he tiny airport emptied and soon I was alone—no people, no cabs, no movement at all. I wasn't even sure I knew the address of where I was going in this strange new country, and I certainly didn't know how I was to get there.

I grumbled to myself. Where was my welcoming committee? I had crossed the ocean with two plane transfers. Here I was, ready to grandmother and teach orphans about the Lord and no one seemed to care.

I felt alone, disconnected from love and hope. I had left my young granddaughter, Aurora, at home in California. I had wondered why the opportunity to fulfill my dream of helping kids overseas had arisen so late in life—right at the time I had grown exceptionally close to Aurora. I could just hear her voice when I would visit her. "Grandma, you're here!" she would exclaim with glee and jump into my arms.

I was losing my granddaughter, I thought with dismay as I sat on a bench, surrounded by my suitcases. My heart ached.

A person stirred within the tiny airport office. I walked over. "Taxi?" I asked in simple English.

"Where go?" the woman replied in broken English.

I fished through my purse for the address. Thankfully, I found it and was soon on my way in the town's only cab.

The guest house at the Bible school campus was empty of people and very hot. Perspiration beaded above my upper lip and dripped down my neck.

Basics, I thought. *Keep your mind on the basics.*

I wandered out to the open street market to buy food and water. Unable to speak the language, I handed the vendor the unfamiliar currency, trusting her to give me back the right change. "Computer? E-mail?" I asked. She just shook her head.

Back at the guest house, I stared at the wall, too cut off from people to even pray to God.

Back home, I lived alone, and when I needed company I watched TV or surfed the Web or drove to my granddaughter's house. When I wanted to talk to friends, I picked up the phone or sent an e-mail or went next door for a cup of tea.

What do you do when you're in a foreign country, have no TV, haven't yet discovered access to Internet or e-mail or phone, can't communicate, don't have friends—and worst of all, don't have your granddaughter?

You cry.

Like rain, tears clear the soul. The next morning, through

more focused vision and the help of Bible school staff, I made contact with the orphanage. In a few days, I boarded an outdated passenger train which nearly bounced off the track. With clunks and clanks, the couplings slammed into each other and rattled my brain. Hot, humid air blew in through the open windows and mixed with the smells of vendors hawking chicken and every kind of produce in the aisles.

When the train made a village whistle stop, I disembarked four feet down, stepping directly into a rice paddy. There I waited on a makeshift bench until a red pickup truck came along the dirt track to get me. We bumped along, passing wooden houses that stood on stilts and water buffalo grazing in the fields.

That's when I met him. The moment I walked into the orphan home, a young boy named Mac who had lost both parents looked up at me with bright eyes and said, "Ma-gee?"

"Yes, I am Ma-gee," I replied with a broad smile. His eager attention made up for my lonely arrival in the country.

Within a couple weeks, the rest of the children moved into the home, and so did I. Like abandoned kittens, the kids seemed so grateful to have a roof over their heads. They came out to greet me with bowed heads and praying hands, the custom. They each picked up one of my possessions and carried it to my room at the back of the compound. Mac led the long procession.

The next morning, Mac was back in action, continuing his loving, helpful ways. He jumped up from his breakfast mat to open the orphan home door for me. When I had trouble taking off my shoes before entering, he steadied my poor balance. When I lacked the flexibility to sit cross-legged on the grass mat on the floor, Mac pulled out a chair for me. When I choked on the hot chili pepper in my fried rice, tomatoes, and egg, he brought me a glass of cool water and another plate without spicy seasoning. He set up my dry-erase board in the classroom and even made it a ritual every night to walk me to my room—despite the monsoons, long-winged flies, and sucking mud.

I wanted to tell him how much he meant to me. But because of the language barrier, I couldn't except through an interpreter, and that didn't seem personal enough. So I took Mac and some other boys to a pizza place in the city, a special treat for them.

Tummies full, their mouths sufficiently scorched—they had smothered the pizza in their favorite hot chili pepper—we walked through the city's first-ever mall. All at once, I felt a hand slip firmly into mine. I looked down. It was Mac's.

In a culture in which touching is only done in families, the gesture said it all: "I want you to be my grandma."

I had come to fulfill a dream and what I felt was a calling

from God to love kids across the globe. And it hadn't been easy for me—I was far away from people I loved and way out of my comfort zone. But with Mac's hand in mine, I knew that I'd been blessed beyond anything I could have imagined: In addition to my lovely granddaughter, I now had a precious, loving grandson on the other side of the world. Mac had shown me what grace really meant, what it really meant to lovingly serve others, and now I had the privilege to call him my "adopted" grandson.

As Mac and I strolled along in a cluster cloud of boys, I felt the soft light of God beam down upon us—and grace abounded in my heart. ✿

Now hope does not disappoint,
because the love of God has been
poured out in our hearts by the
Holy Spirit who was given to us.

ROMANS 5:5

Every Kingdom work,
whether publicly performed
or privately endeavored,
partakes of the Kingdom's
imperishable character.

BRUCE MILNE

Who Blessed Whom?

DIANE H. PITTS

*D*o you think you can help Alex?" my friend Lisa asked.

The answer changed my life—as a physical therapist and as a person.

Lisa and Keith Coggin sponsored a young man named Alex who lived in a Ugandan orphanage. Because of malnutrition, Alex looked fourteen rather than seventeen, and he was scarred from chronic bone infections and surgery. Lisa wanted to bring him to the United States for hip replacement surgery and physical therapy. Would I help them navigate the medical system and handle his therapy?

I was honored to do so.

The first time I saw Alex, he smiled as broad as the African plains. He leaned heavily on makeshift crutches, and his ebony eyes connected with mine.

"Aunt Diane," he asked, using a term of respect, "will you help me walk better?"

My stomach tightened. Four years ago, I'd walked away from my physical therapy practice, yet here was a young man asking me to give again, to get involved. I heard myself say,

"Alex, I'll try."

Over the next few weeks, we shuttled between doctor's offices. Finally, we consulted with a bone specialist, who got straight to the point.

"Alex, your hip is much worse than the X-rays from Africa indicated. There's no place to attach a new joint." He looked absent and began shuffling papers. "If there was any chance at all, I'd do it."

Alex nodded and looked at the floor. "Thank you, sir."

His sadness touched me deeply. *Why, God?* I prayed. *Our hopes were so high. How could You bring him this far to hit a brick wall?*

We drove in silence back to the Coggins' house. Over the next few days, Alex grappled with disappointment only to face another blow: He developed a high fever because of an infection in his right foot. We went back to the doctor for high-powered antibiotics and outpatient surgery to clean the wound. Despite these obstacles, Alex studied ten, sometimes twelve, hours a day for his exams back home.

"Mama," my three boys asked, "why does Alex study so hard?"

"Education is the only way he can survive in Uganda. He's on his own and has to earn a living." I smiled and ruffled the hair of my oldest son, Jacob. "Unfortunately, Alex doesn't have a mom to give him a hard time and tell him to get to work."

Jacob, Tyler, and John looked at me, wide-eyed. "But, Mom, he has you."

My throat constricted. "Yeah, guys, I guess he does." From Lisa's kitchen I watched Alex study. His leg was swathed in white bandages; books surrounded him on the sofa. There was no one else in the world like Alex, I was sure.

One afternoon, I took Alex to wound care at a local hospital. With the roar of the whirlpool in the background, Alex studied, and the therapist motioned me to the other side of the room so we could discuss his progress. Glancing at him, then at me, she whispered, "He's like a little Christ, isn't he?"

He was. He gave grace to everyone in his path. His character shone bright under adversity. Even someone who didn't know Christ could recognize His resemblance.

When Alex's wound healed and the infection came under control, I worked with him to stretch and strengthen the muscles. I actually enjoyed using the skills I had shelved like books. Some days I cried when we gained half an inch of stretch. Alex just smiled and said, "I told you God would do this."

Although he didn't get a new hip joint during his time in the States as was the original plan, over the next six months Alex progressed from two crutches to a cane. And I too progressed by regaining my passion to help.

As the time neared for Alex to return home, I approached him one day about going to school in the States, offering to host him in our home while he studied. His face showed conflicting emotions.

"Aunt Diane ... in this country, citizens have everything. In Uganda we have nothing. If I stayed, I would get lazy; things are too easy here. The Lord Jesus wants me to go back and tell my people what He can do."

I couldn't believe what I was hearing. We were offering him better healthcare and an escape from poverty. I shuddered—death was a very real risk if he returned to Uganda, where medical care was scarce. His response shook me on the deepest level.

I could see the truth of what he was saying. Recent scenes slipped through my mind, and I knew Alex had been tested here. Not immune to peer pressure, he had a hard time wearing a built-up shoe when he could get name-brand shoes and be "cool" like the other kids. He enjoyed spending money at the mall and was quite the bargain hunter.

His voice burst into my thoughts. "I have to go back to Uganda. Perhaps you will come, and I will show you my home." His familiar grin warmed my aching heart, and I knew I had to let him go.

Within a week, the Coggins and Alex boarded a plane to Uganda. I plunged back into my pre-Alex daily schedule, but my thoughts were consumed with how Alex had touched so many people—the church youth group, the hospital staff, and especially me—with the grace of God.

Two weeks after he returned to Uganda, Alex was stricken with a raging fever that did not yield to medication. One might, he lay on the floor praying and repeating Scripture, asking his Father to intervene. By morning, God had healed Alex of the fever.

When I heard the story, my body went cold. I heard God's heart: *You blessed Alex with your care, but do you see that healing is ultimately in My hand?* In that moment, I knew that the Lord wanted me not to waste the lessons He'd used Alex to teach me, that He wanted me to use my skills again to share His grace through compassionate health care.

My hands touched the broken body of an African boy, but through his life, God touched my heart with grace. ✿

Brethren, the grace of our
Lord Jesus Christ be with your spirit.

GALATIANS 6:18

*Our happiness is greatest
when we contribute most
to the happiness of others.*

HARRIET SHEPARD

The Surprise Gifts

EVA JULIUSON

Walking out of my husband's hospital room, ~~I was~~ *I was* ~~more despondent than ever~~. Struggling to balance the infant carrier that held our three month-old baby and all the paraphernalia that must go everywhere with a new infant, I paused to shift everything and grab five-year-old Ryan's hand.

He was always quiet. He had learned to be silent, just so he could be around his dad, who had been deathly sick for the past three years. Ryan's young eyes had seen more suffering than most people do all their lives. The past month had been the worst yet.

As we made our way past the nurses' station, my eyes caught sight of the brightly colored Christmas decorations. I couldn't believe it—Christmas was only a few days away.

It certainly didn't feel like Christmas. Christmas had always meant a huge celebration for our family. As we rode the elevator down, carefree memories of past holiday fun rolled around in my head—stark contrast to the sterile hospital environment where we'd inevitably be spending the holiday.

With my husband being so seriously ill, how could I help him or our four children experience Christmas? We had absolutely no money. Without insurance, Steve's medical bills and prescriptions left us swimming in a sea of financial problems. But worst of all was our emotional state. How could we celebrate when everything seemed so hopeless? But as we walked out to the car, I had an idea—we could give gifts to a family who didn't have any.

Every year we'd been married, we had bought presents for a family who couldn't afford to buy gifts for the kids. And every year, that's what had really put us into the Christmas spirit. That's what we'd do! We couldn't buy new gifts, but I knew we could come up with something we had at home. My excitement started to grow. By the time we arrived home, I remembered my girlfriend telling me about a young family living nearby who didn't have anything for Christmas. That's who we would surprise.

When I told my two older kids what I was dreaming, they caught my excitement, and we searched our whole house for anything that would make a good gift. I found a full bottle of perfume and a bracelet for the mom. Eric, my oldest son, found a really cool car and a game for the boy. My daughter, Chrissy, came out of her room with some stuffed animals, a doll, and a glittery little purse for the girl. Ryan had some clothes that were like new and were just the right size for the boy. And in the hall closet, we discovered a whole box of wrapping paper left over from last year.

Our house was filled with giggles as we all pitched in to wrap the packages. The kids made cards to attach to each gift that said, "From: Guess who?" Eric found a big box to put all the gifts in. Someone had brought us a basketful of fruit and nuts, so we added a few of those to the box.

As I bundled the baby in the car, the kids worked as a team to load the box of goodies into the back seat. When we got to their apartment, we checked carefully to make sure no one was watching. The kids grabbed the box and hurriedly placed it in front of the door. Chrissy rang the doorbell, and then they all ran as fast as their legs would carry them back to the "getaway car" where I waited.

As soon as the doors on the car shut, I sped away, and we saw the apartment door open as our tires squealed down the street. We had done it! There was more laughter and sheer joy in that car than there had been in a long time. Each of the kids breathlessly reported to me how they almost got caught and how they wished they could see the kids' faces when they opened the gifts. I told the kids that this was what Christmas was all about: God had blessed us and wanted us to give something of ourselves to someone who needed it. We all felt

B & Marie

so good to be able to share with someone else who was having a hard time. It was our Christmas gift to God.

Our faces were still glowing with smiles when we got home. I stopped to check the mailbox. The mail hadn't come yet, but there were six envelopes inside, one for each of us, with our names printed on the outside. I curiously opened mine and discovered a $100 gift certificate for clothes.

Each of the kids found the same gift in their envelope. I couldn't believe it—and I couldn't wait to tell my husband. The Christmas spirit had indeed descended upon my family.

<u>We wanted to give something of ourselves for the Lord, but</u> <u>He gave us even more.</u> ✸

God supplies all our needs. *Phil 4/19*

Cast all your care upon Him for He cares for us. *1 Peter 5/7*

> *Good will come to him*
> *who is generous and lends freely,*
> *who conducts his affairs with justice.*
>
> PSALM 112:5 NIV

Prayer next page

Prayer

Teach us, Lord, to serve You as You deserve,
to give and not to count the cost,
to fight and not to heed the wounds,
to toil and not to seek for rest,
to labor and not to ask for any reward
save that of knowing that we do Your will.

IGNATIUS LOYOLA

Ministering to Jesus

CHRISTY PHILLIPPE

As Penelope walked across the parking lot one hot August afternoon, she prayed that God would use her to bring His love to her patients. As a registered nurse, she had many opportunities to pray for patients and their families and for the opportunity to be a vessel for God's use. Her heart was hurting that particular day for one of her patients: a young man with a precious wife and a dear little towheaded two-year-old son.

Donald had been diagnosed with leukemia about a year before, and the nursing staff had witnessed his body's gradual decline. Now he was in his last days, and his beautiful young wife remained by his bedside. She would slip out of his room frequently, lean against the wall, and weep. If their little two-year-old was there, he would wrap his chubby arms around her legs and ask, "Mommy, why are you sad?"

When Donald was first admitted to the hospital, he had been pleasant and friendly, but with each successive admission for chemotherapy, he became more angry and withdrawn. Each visit kept him longer and longer, and whenever he was Penelope's patient, she prayed, "God, give me the right words to say, and help him to be open to hearing about You." He always remained polite but curt, and left very little opportunity for her to share with him.

That morning at church, the guest speaker had shared from Matthew 25 and talked about how when God's servants minister to other people, they also minister to Jesus. Penelope could understand the idea of blessing other people with Jesus, but she was not too clear about ministering to Him. So she prayed that morning for God to show her how to minister to and bless Him. But that was the farthest thing from her mind as she arrived at work.

That evening after arriving, Penelope started going from room to room, getting her assigned patients ready for the night. She came to Donald's room, and as she passed under the doorway, she prayed, "Please, God, open Donald's heart and let me minister to him." She had a feeling this might be her last chance. He was now only skin and bones, every vertebra and joint showing through his transparent skin. The room was dim and quiet, except for his labored breathing. Penelope gave him his medications, hung a new IV bottle, and straightened his bed.

"Donald," she quietly said, "what can I do to make you more comfortable?"

He replied in a soft, raspy whisper, more like a man of

advanced years than a man in his late twenties. "Please, could you rub my back? It hurts so much."

As Penelope carefully rubbed lotion on Donald's back, she began to pray for him, and again prayed for the right words. Nothing. She closed her eyes and focused on Jesus as she kept massaging his fragile back. Donald seemed to be relaxing a little, his breathing quieter and slower. A feeling of peacefulness invaded the room. And deep within her soul, Penelope was filled with an awareness that this was Jesus' striped back she was massaging, His body she was lovingly caring for. When she opened her eyes, it was like she saw Jesus lying there, and that sweet peace continued to permeate the air.

By now he had fallen asleep, and Penelope quietly left the room, quietly thanking the Lord.

Penelope had been a grace giver that day, and she had received an amazing blessing in return. She had said more to Donald by her actions than by words. In that moment, Penelope learned that when we are available and willing to serve other people, we are truly ministering to Jesus. ✪

The King will reply, "I tell you the truth, whatever you did for one of the least of these brothers of mine, you did for me.

MATTHEW 25:40 NIV

One can never pay in gratitude;
one can only pay "in kind"
somewhere else in life.

ANNE MORROW LINDBERGH

Miracle at the Cromwell Crown Hotel

HARRY HEINTZ AS TOLD TO PEGGY FREZON

We'd been roaming the city for hours, dragging heavy suitcases and anxiously searching for a place to stay. Eighteen members of my church and I were on our way home to New York from a mission trip in Nairobi, Kenya. After an eight-hour flight, we touched down at Heathrow, ready for a few days of rest in London before continuing on to New York. We were tired, but also scared. Just a few hours earlier as we were riding toward King's Cross station on the Piccadilly subway line (locally called "the tube"), everything ground to a halt.

Workers urgently directed us to evacuate the subway immediately. Confused, we joined the throng of passengers crushing out the doors and spilling onto the streets. Hundreds of others, also evacuated from their trains, ran up and down the sidewalks. It looked like a scene from an action movie. Sirens blared and traffic tangled in all directions. *Dear Lord, what has happened here?* I wondered.

"What's going on?" I asked everyone I saw. Before long, we found out.

"A bomb!" someone said.

"Terrorist bombings," another passerby explained with wide eyes. "One bomb blew up a double-decker bus. Another went off at the King's Cross station."

King's Cross—right where we had been headed. We were only a handful of stops away. If we had been a few minutes earlier, our trip would have taken a sudden and tragic turn.

The subways were down, all buses had stopped running, and taxis and car rentals were nowhere to be found. After walking and lugging our bags for hours, we realized there was no way we could get across town to our hotel. We needed a place to rest, regroup, and get in touch with our families across the Atlantic. With the afternoon waning, we'd have to settle for anything we could find.

"Do you have any rooms?" I asked over and over, my voice growing hoarse. We were turned away everywhere. We could only find vacancies in large hotels with sky-high prices, far out of reach on our modest budget. When we passed a small hotel—the Cromwell Crown—something told me to give it a try.

"We've been wandering for hours," I told the lady behind the desk. "We've just returned from a mission trip in Kenya and we're very tired. Can you help us?"

As I explained my plight to the desk clerk, a man stepped next to me, seemingly out of nowhere. His expressive, dark eyes revealed that he understood our predicament. "What can you afford?" he asked.

"Not much," I replied soberly.

He looked at us thoughtfully for a moment and then nodded. "I can help."

I didn't quite believe it. "Thank you so much, sir. We are so very grateful," I said, finally releasing my heavy bags, wanting to hug him.

But his response surprised me. "No, I am grateful. It is my turn to help you," he said. "You see, I am from Kenya."

It had been an honor to serve in Kenya, and we had been more than compensated by the loving gratitude of the people we served there. But through this man's generosity, God showed us again that our efforts had mattered. Just when we needed it most, when the city's peace was shattered and our nerves were raw, we felt God's touch and blessing. ❁

"So which of these three do you think was a neighbor to him
who fell among the thieves?" And he said, "He who showed
mercy on him." Then Jesus said to him, "Go and do likewise."

LUKE 10:36-37

Acknowledgements

"Answered Prayer at the Fair" © Christy Phillippe. Used by permission. All rights reserved.

"The Birthday Gift" © Judith Scharfenberg. Used by permission. All rights reserved.

"Caregiver of the Century" © Katherine J. Crawford. Used by permission. All rights reserved.

"A Cup of Hope" © Beverly Hill McKinney. Used by permission. All rights reserved.

"A Cry for Mercy" © Nanette Thorsen-Snipes. Used by permission. All rights reserved.

"Dinner with Sinners" © Tonya Ruiz. Used by permission. All rights reserved.

"A Dream Come True" © Christy Phillippe. Used by permission. All rights reserved.

"Forgive? Who, Me?" © Candy Arrington. Used by permission. All rights reserved.

"Giving Brings Healing" © Sharon Gibson. Used by permission. All rights reserved.

"God's Thread" © Heidi Shelton-Jenck. Used by permission. All rights reserved.

"A God Nearby" © Christy Phillippe. Used by permission. All rights reserved.

"Going Global" © Jessica Inman. Used by permission. All rights reserved.

"Graced and Gracious" © David Jeremiah. Used by permission. All rights reserved.

"Green Ink" © Laura L. Smith. Used by permission. All rights reserved.

"His Grace Is Sufficient" © David Jeremiah. Used by permission. All rights reserved.

"Hope Does Not Disappoint" © Margaret Lang. Used by permission. All rights reserved.

"Hospital Maneuvers" © Betty Winslow. Used by permission. All rights reserved.

"I Simply Let Go" © Karen O'Connor. Used by permission. All rights reserved.

"In Jesus' Name" © Christy Phillippe. Used by permission. All rights reserved.

"Itty-Bitty Woman" © Candy Arrington. Used by permission. All rights reserved.